Show me

MW01143308

Windows 3.1

A Visual Guide to the Basics

Michael Griffin

| File | Edit | View | Layout | Tool |

1   2   3   4   5   6

New
Open
Retrieve
Close
Save
Run
Save As

File Manager

alpha
books

A Division of Prentice Hall Computer Publishing
1711 North College Avenue, Carmel, Indiana 46032 USA

International Standard Book Number: 1-56761-236-9
Library of Congress Catalog Card Number: 93-71227

95 94 93   8 7 6 5 4 3 2 1

Interpretation of the printing code: the rightmost number of the first series of numbers is the year of the book's printing; the rightmost number of the second series of numbers is the number of the book's printing. For example, a printing code of 93-1 shows that the first printing of the book occurred in 1993.

Screen reproductions in this book were created by means of the program Collage Plus from Inner Media, Inc., Hollis, NH.

Printed in the United States of America

TRADEMARKS

Publisher
Marie Butler-Knight

Associate Publisher
Lisa A. Bucki

Managing Editor
Elizabeth Keaffaber

Acquisitions Manager
Stephen R. Poland

Development Editor
Seta Frantz

Manuscript Editor
San Dee Phillips

Cover Designer
Scott Fullmer

Designer
Roger Morgan

Indexer
Jeanne Clark

Production Team
*Diana Bigham, Katy Bodenmiller, Scott Cook, Tim Cox,
Mark Enochs, Linda Koopman, Tom Loveman,
Joe Ramon, Carrie Roth, Greg Simsic*

*Special thanks to Kelly Oliver and C. Herbert Feltner for
ensuring the technical accuracy of this book.*

CONTENTS

INTRODUCTION

Have you ever said to yourself, "I wish someone would just *show me* how to use Windows." If you have, this *Show Me* book is for you. In it, you won't find detailed explanations of what's going on in your computer each time you enter a command. Instead, you will see pictures that *show you*, step by step, how to perform a particular task.

This book will make you feel as though you have your very own personal trainer standing next to you, pointing at the screen and showing you exactly what to do.

WHAT IS WINDOWS?

The Microsoft Windows 3.1 is an operating environment that makes your computer easier to use. If you have worked with DOS (disk operating system), you will find Windows more intuitive and efficient to use than DOS. You don't have to remember to type a DOS command in a specified way. Instead, Windows uses a visual approach to tasks. You tell the computer what to do by choosing commands from menus, selecting buttons, and choosing small pictures called icons. You can perform these actions with your mouse or keyboard.

The Windows format is consistent from one program to another. By learning how to use one Windows application, you learn fundamentals that are useful when using other Windows applications. Applications are programs, such as a word processing, spreadsheet, or database program.

The best way to describe the look of Windows is to say that it is a desktop of windows, command menus, and icons.

Windows are rectangular shaped areas which can contain applications, icons, and documents that you are creating. *Icons* are small pictures that represent a group of programs, an application, or a file created by an application. For example, a Windows application called File Manager is represented by an icon that looks like a filing cabinet.

The foundation of the Windows program is the Program Manager. You use the Program Manager to organize applications into logical groups, to start programs, and to exit from Windows. No matter what it is you are doing with Windows, the Program Manager is always present. When you start Windows, the Program Manager is automatically up and running and it is the first thing you see.

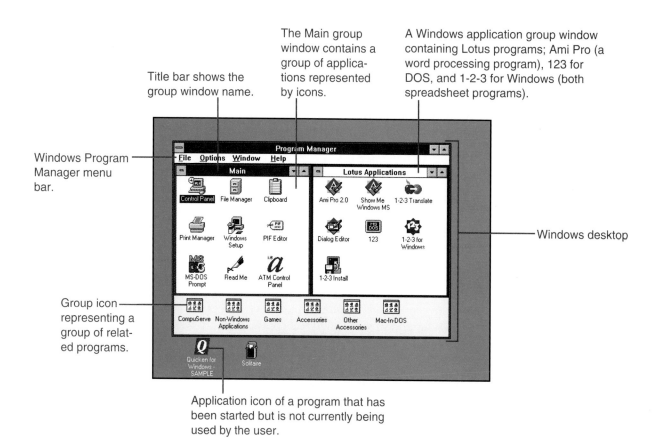

Title bar shows the group window name.

The Main group window contains a group of applications represented by icons.

A Windows application group window containing Lotus programs; Ami Pro (a word processing program), 123 for DOS, and 1-2-3 for Windows (both spreadsheet programs).

Windows Program Manager menu bar.

Windows desktop

Group icon representing a group of related programs.

Application icon of a program that has been started but is not currently being used by the user.

HOW TO USE THIS BOOK

Using this book is as simple as falling off your chair. Just flip to the task that you want to perform and follow the steps. You will see easy step-by-step instructions that tell you which keys to press and which commands to select. You will also see step-by-step pictures that show you what to do. Follow the steps or the pictures (or both) to complete the task. Here's an example of a set of instructions from this book.

Saving a Document

1 Click on **File**, or press **Alt+F**.

2 Click on Save As, or press **A**.

3 Type a filename in the File Name text box.

4 In the **Directories** list box, click on the directory to which you want to save the file. If you are using the keyboard, press **Alt+D**, and use the down arrow key to select a directory.

5 If you want to save on another drive, click on the Drives drop-down list box, and click on a drive. If you are using the keyboard, press **Alt+V**, and use the up and down arrow keys to select a drive.

6 Click on the **OK** button, or press **ENTER**.

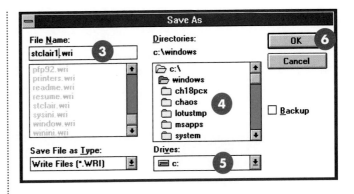

Every computer book has its own way of telling you which buttons to push and which keys to press. Here's how this book handles those formalities:

- Keys that you should press appear as they do on your keyboard (for example, press **Alt** or press **F10**). If you need to press more than one key at once, the keys are separated with plus signs. For example, if the text tells you to press **Alt+F**, hold down the **Alt** key while pressing the **F** key.

- Text that you should type is printed in **boldface type like this**.

- Some features are activated by selecting a menu and then a command. If I tell you to "select **File New**," you should open the **File** menu and select the **New** command. In this book, the selection letter is printed in boldface for easy recognition.

Definitions in Plain English

In addition to the basic step-by-step approach, pages may contain Learn the Lingo definitions to help you understand key terms. These definitions are placed off to the side, so you can easily skip them.

LEARNING THE LINGO

Pull-down menu: A menu that appears at the top of the screen, listing various commands. The menu is not visible until you select it from the menu bar. The menu then drops down, covering a small part of the screen.

3

Quick Refreshers

If you need to know how to perform some other task in order to perform the current task, look for a Quick Refresher. With the Quick Refresher, you won't have to flip through the book to learn how to perform the other task; the information is right where you need it.

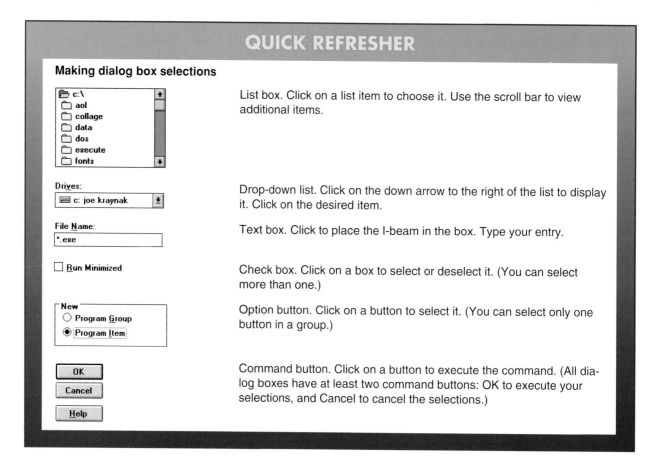

QUICK REFRESHER

Making dialog box selections

List box. Click on a list item to choose it. Use the scroll bar to view additional items.

Drop-down list. Click on the down arrow to the right of the list to display it. Click on the desired item.

Text box. Click to place the I-beam in the box. Type your entry.

Check box. Click on a box to select or deselect it. (You can select more than one.)

Option button. Click on a button to select it. (You can select only one button in a group.)

Command button. Click on a button to execute the command. (All dialog boxes have at least two command buttons: OK to execute your selections, and Cancel to cancel the selections.)

Tips, Ideas, and Shortcuts

Throughout this book, you will encounter tips that provide important information about a task or tell you how to perform the task more quickly.

TIP

A shortcut way to exit Windows is to double-click the Control Menu box or press **Alt+F4**.

If you change your mind and do not want to end your Windows session, click on the **Cancel** button in the Exit Windows Dialog Box, or press **ESC**.

Exercises

Because most people learn by doing, several exercises throughout the book give you additional practice performing a task.

Exercise

Follow these steps to make a directory at the DOS prompt, change to the directory, and delete it:

1 Type **cd**, and press **Enter** to change to the root directory.

2 Type **md testdir**, and press **Enter** to make the TESTDIR directory.

3 Type **cd\testdir**, and press **Enter** to change to the TEST-DIR directory.

4 Type **cd**, and press **Enter** to change back to the root directory.

5 Type **rd testdir**, and press **Enter** to remove the TESTDIR directory.

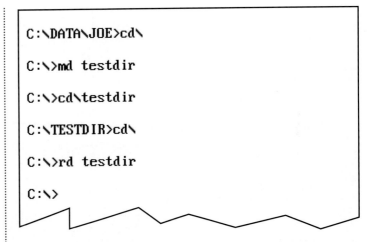

```
C:\DATA\JOE>cd\

C:\>md testdir

C:\>cd\testdir

C:\TESTDIR>cd\

C:\>rd testdir

C:\>
```

Where Should You Start?

If this is your first encounter with computers, read the next section, "Quick Computer Tour," before reading anything else. This section explains some computer basics that you need to know in order to get your computer up and running.

Once you know the basics, you can work through this book from beginning to end or skip around from task to task, as needed. If you decide to skip around, there are several ways you can find what you're looking for:

- Use the Table of Contents at the front of this book to find a specific task you want to perform.

- Use the complete index at the back of this book to look up a specific task or topic and find the page number on which it is covered.

- Use the color-coded sections to find groups of related tasks.

- Flip through the book and look at the task titles at the top of the pages. This method works best if you know the general location of the task in the book.

- Use the inside back cover of this book to quickly find the page on which a command you are looking for is covered.

QUICK COMPUTER TOUR

If this is your first time in front of a computer, the next few sections will teach you the least you need to know to get started.

Parts of a Computer

Think of a computer as a car. The system unit holds the engine that powers the computer. The monitor is like the windshield that lets you see where you're going. And the keyboard and mouse are like the steering wheel, which allow you to control the computer.

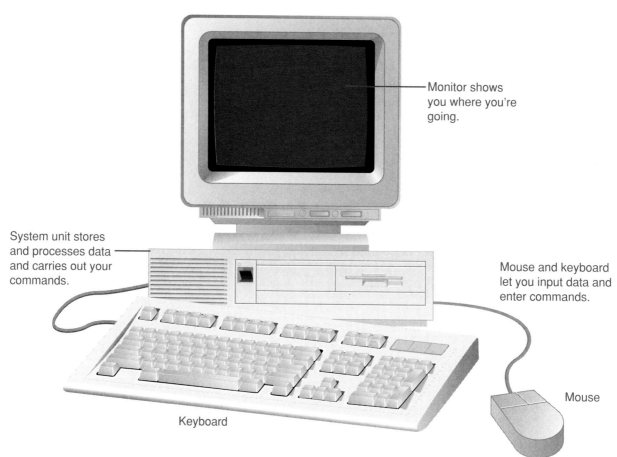

Monitor shows you where you're going.

System unit stores and processes data and carries out your commands.

Mouse and keyboard let you input data and enter commands.

Mouse

Keyboard

The System Unit

The system unit contains three basic elements: a central processing unit (CPU), which does all the "thinking" for the computer; random-access memory (RAM), which stores instructions and data while the CPU is processing it; and disk drives, which store information permanently on disks to keep the information safe. It also contains several ports (at the back), which allow you to connect other devices to it, such as a keyboard, mouse, and printer.

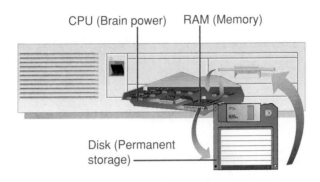

CPU (Brain power)   RAM (Memory)

Disk (Permanent storage)

Using a Keyboard

The keyboard is no mystery. It contains a set of alphanumeric (letter and number) keys for entering text, arrow keys for moving around on-screen, and function keys (F1, F2, and so on) for entering commands. It also has some odd keys, including Alt (Alternative), Ctrl (Control), and Esc (Escape) that perform special actions.

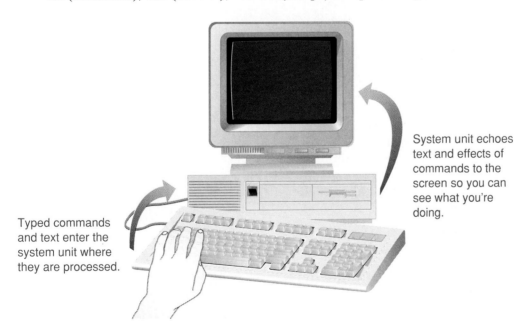

System unit echoes text and effects of commands to the screen so you can see what you're doing.

Typed commands and text enter the system unit where they are processed.

Using a Mouse

Like the keyboard, a mouse allows you to communicate with the computer. You roll the mouse around on your desk to move a *mouse pointer* on the screen. You can use the pointer to open menus and select other items on-screen. Here are some mouse techniques you must master:

Pointing. To point, roll the mouse on your desk until the tip of the mouse pointer is on the item to which you want to point.

Clicking. To click on an item, point to the desired item, and then hold the mouse steady while you press and release the mouse button. Use the left mouse button unless I tell you specifically to use the right button.

Double-clicking. To double-click, hold the mouse steady while you press and release the mouse button twice quickly.

Right-clicking. To right-click, click using the right mouse button instead of the left button.

Understanding Disks, Directories, and Files

Whatever you type (a letter, a list of names, a tax return) is stored only in your computer's temporary memory and is erased when the electricity is turned off. To protect your work, you must save it in a *file* on a *disk*.

A *file* is like a folder that you might use to store a report or a letter. You name the file, so you can later find and retrieve the information it contains.

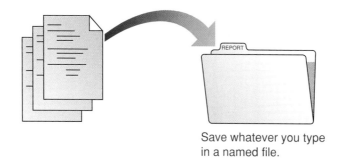

Save whatever you type in a named file.

Files are stored on *disks*. Your computer probably has a *hard disk* inside it (called drive C) to which you can save your files. You can also save files to *floppy disks*, which you insert into the slots (the floppy disk drives) on the front of the computer.

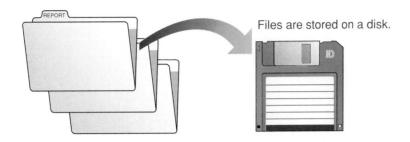

Files are stored on a disk.

To keep files organized on a disk, you can create *directories* on the disk. Each directory acts as a drawer in a filing cabinet, storing a group of related files. Although you can create directories on both floppy and hard disks, most people use directories only on hard disks.

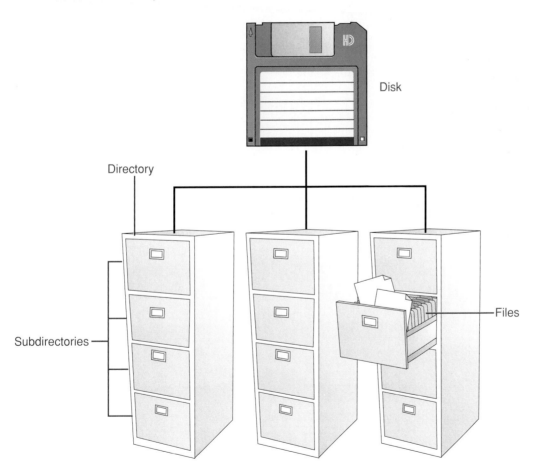

PART 1

BEGINNING WINDOWS TASKS

In this section, you will learn the basic tasks necessary to begin using Microsoft Windows 3.1. Once you have finished working through this section, you will be able to start up Windows, open menus, get help, and exit Windows.

- Starting Windows

- Choosing Menu Commands

- Working with Dialog Boxes

- Using Scroll Bars

- Opening Control Menus

- Getting Help

- Exiting Windows

STARTING WINDOWS

Why Start Windows?

Starting Windows loads the program into your computer's memory and places the Windows desktop on your screen. Every time you load Windows, you'll see the Program Manager appear on your screen. The Program Manager is the main Windows program that lets you run all other applications.

Before you can start Windows 3.1, it must be installed on your hard disk. To install Windows, refer to the installation instructions found at the end of this book.

LEARNING THE LINGO

Hard disk: The permanent storage area of your computer. You can use the hard disk just as you would use floppy disks—to save files and store applications.

Memory: The working storage area of your computer. The size of your computer's memory, also referred to as RAM (random access memory) determines the size and number of applications that you can run at the same time and the amount of data your computer can process.

Desktop: The screen areas on which windows and icons are displayed.

Program Manager: The foundation of a Windows program which you can use to organize applications into logical groups, to start programs, and to exit from Windows. When you start Windows, Program Manager is automatically up and running and it is the first thing you see.

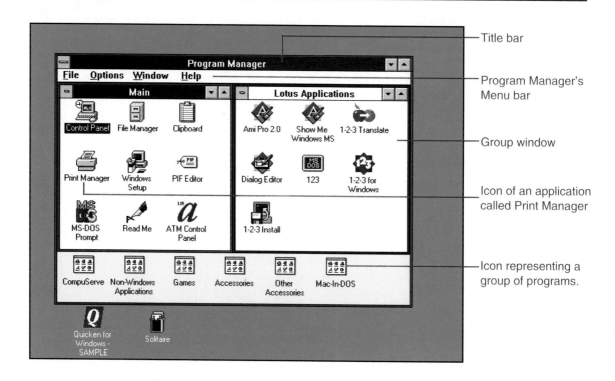

Title bar

Program Manager's Menu bar

Group window

Icon of an application called Print Manager

Icon representing a group of programs.

Starting Windows

1 Turn on your computer and monitor.

2 At the DOS prompt, which looks like **C:\>**, **C:**, or **C:**, type **win**.

3 Press **Enter**.

TIP

If you type **win** at the DOS prompt and you get a **bad command or filename** message, try typing **cd\windows** to switch to the Windows directory, and then type **win** and press return. Also, depending on how your system is set up, Windows may start up automatically when you turn on your computer.

TIP

To have Windows start automatically when you turn on your computer, add the line **win** at the end of your AUTOEXEC.BAT file (caution: make a backup copy of your current AUTOEXEC.BAT file, in case you encounter problems when editing). When you start your computer, it automatically runs DOS, and then DOS runs the commands contained in the AUTOEXEC.BAT file. The AUTOEXEC.BAT file, also known as a *batch file*, is a file that tells DOS to execute a set of commands each time you turn on your computer. To edit the AUTOEXEC.BAT file, use a text editor, like Notepad (a Windows Accessories application). If you are not sure how to do any of the things I described, you may want to seek out a DOS expert to help you.

Beginning Windows Tasks

CHOOSING MENU COMMANDS

Why Use Menus?

In Windows, you choose commands and tasks to perform by selecting them from menus. For example, to exit Windows, you have to choose the Exit command from the File menu before you can exit. The easiest way to select a menu is by using the mouse. However, you can use the keyboard to select menus and choose commands.

You will see that menu commands can contain a check mark, ellipsis (...), triangle, key combinations and some items that may be dimmed. All of these characters mean something. Here's an explanation of the menu conventions:

Cut Ctrl+X	A dimmed command means that the command is not available.
Links...	Ellipsis (...) following a command means that a dialog box will appear when you choose the command.
√ Single Space 1 1/2 Space Double Space	A check mark next to a command means that the command has been activated.
Undo Editing Ctrl+Z	A key combination beside a command means there is a keyboard shortcut for choosing the command.

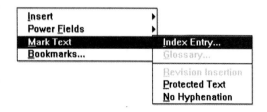

A triangle beside a command means a cascading menu appears when you choose the command.

Choosing a Menu Command

1 Move the mouse pointer and point to the name of the menu on the menu bar, or press the **Alt** or **F10** key.

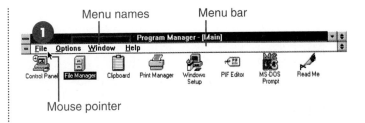

Menu names   Menu bar

Mouse pointer

2 Click the mouse button to open a menu, or if you are using the keyboard, press Alt and the selection letter (underlined letter).

3 Click on the menu command of choice, or if you are using the keyboard, press the selection letter.

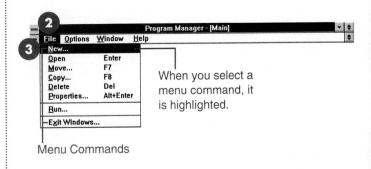

When you select a menu command, it is highlighted.

Menu Commands

LEARNING THE LINGO

Dialog boxes: Windows that appear to request additional information or additional command options. In addition, a dialog box may ask you to confirm that you want a particular command carried out and may remind you of the consequences of the command.

Cascading menu: A menu that opens from a command of another menu.

Key combinations: Two keys that you press together to execute a task.

Selection letter: The underlined letter of a command menu choice.

Command: A word or phrase in a menu that you select to carry out a task.

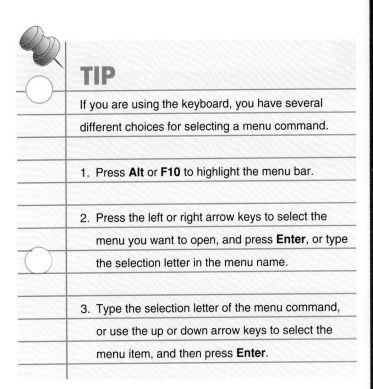

TIP

If you are using the keyboard, you have several different choices for selecting a menu command.

1. Press **Alt** or **F10** to highlight the menu bar.

2. Press the left or right arrow keys to select the menu you want to open, and press **Enter**, or type the selection letter in the menu name.

3. Type the selection letter of the menu command, or use the up or down arrow keys to select the menu item, and then press **Enter**.

Beginning Windows Tasks

CHOOSING MENU COMMANDS

Exercise

To practice selecting commands from menus, choose the **W**indow menu on the menu bar, and select Accessories to open the Accessories group window.

1 Point to the **W**indow menu, or press **Alt** or **F10** to activate the menu bar.

2 Click the mouse button, or press **W** to open the **W**indow menu.

3 Select Accessories by clicking on it or using the arrow keys to highlight it and pressing **Enter**.

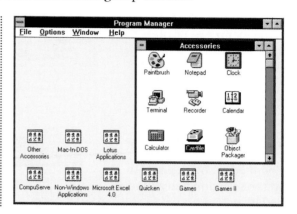

QUICK REFRESHER

Point: Move the mouse, positioning the mouse pointer on an item of choice.

Click: Press and release the left mouse button.

Drag: Point to an item, then press and hold the left mouse button as you move the mouse, dragging the item around the display. When finished dragging, release the mouse button.

WORKING WITH DIALOG BOXES

Why Use Dialog Boxes?

A dialog box is a window that is displayed on the screen when it needs some information from you. A dialog box is often displayed when you select a menu command. While every dialog box is different, they all share the same common components. If you learn how to use these components, you'll be able to use any dialog box you encounter.

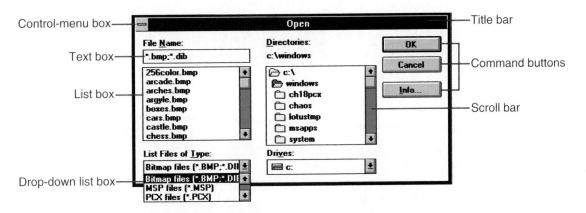

Control-menu box — Title bar
Text box — Command buttons
List box — Scroll bar
Drop-down list box —

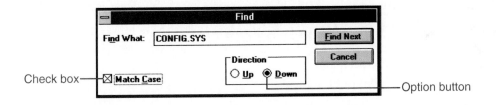

Check box — Option button

TIP

Once a dialog box is open, you may want to move it so that you can view other information on the screen. To move the dialog box, point to the title bar of the dialog box; click and hold the mouse button while you move (drag) the dialog box to a new location. To close a dialog box, choose the **Cancel** button or double-click on the **Control**-menu box of the dialog box.

Selecting Dialog Box Options

List box: Click on a list item to choose it, and use the scroll bars to view other list items. Or if you are using the keyboard, press **TAB** or **Alt** and the selection letter in the option name, and press the up and down arrow keys.

Drop Down list box: Click on the down arrow to the right of the list to display it, and click on an item. If you are using the keyboard, you can press **TAB** or **Alt** and the selection letter in the option name, and press the down arrow key.

Check box: Click on a box to select or deselect an option. If you are using the kcyboard, you can press **TAB** or **Alt** and the selection letter in the option name.

Option button: Click on a button to select or deselect an option. If you are using the keyboard, you can press **TAB** or **Alt** and the selection letter in the option name.

Command button: Click on a button to execute or cancel the dialog selections. If you are using the keyboard, you can press **TAB** or **Alt** and the selection letter in the command button name. The OK and Cancel command buttons do not have selection letters. Press **Enter** to execute the OK button and **Esc** to Cancel.

SCROLLING

When to Use Scroll Bars

Some dialog boxes and other windows have scroll bars that you can use to view information that is contained beyond the visible parts of the window. There will be times when the information in a list box or window is too long or wide to fit into the window or list box. With scroll bars, you can view this hidden information by moving the bars vertically or horizontally.

Scroll bar can be used to view the list.

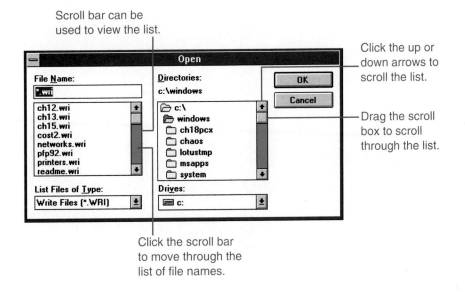

Click the up or down arrows to scroll the list.

Drag the scroll box to scroll through the list.

Click the scroll bar to move through the list of file names.

LEARNING THE LINGO

Scroll: To move through parts of a window to view additional information.

Scroll bar: A bar that appears at the right edge or the bottom of a window whose contents may not be entirely visible.

Beginning Windows Tasks

19

Scrolling

1 Point to the scroll box arrows, and click and hold on one of the arrows. If you are using the keyboard, press the arrow key that points to the direction you want to scroll.

2 With the mouse, drag the box up or down to move through the window. When you are at the location you want, release the mouse button.

TIP

You can also scroll a window one line or screen at a time. To scroll one line at a time, click the up or down scroll arrow. To scroll one screen, click on the scroll bar above or below the scroll box on a vertical scroll bar, and to the left or right of the scroll box on a horizontal scroll bar. If you are using the keyboard, you can move one line up or down by pressing the up or down arrow keys, and one screen by pressing the Page Up or Page Down keys.

OPENING CONTROL MENUS

When to Open Control Menus

All dialog boxes, windows, and icons have Control menus. The Control menu allows you to manipulate dialog boxes, windows, and icons so you can control how they appear on your Windows desktop. You are able to maximize, minimize, restore, move and size windows, close, and switch between open windows.

LEARNING THE LINGO

Control menu: Menu of commands to manipulate windows, dialog boxes, and icons (that is, restore, move, size, and close).

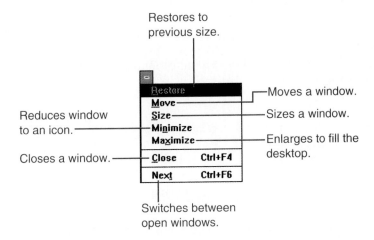

Restores to previous size.

Reduces window to an icon.

Closes a window.

Moves a window.

Sizes a window.

Enlarges to fill the desktop.

Switches between open windows.

Opening the Control Menu for a Window or Dialog Box

1 Click the Control box in the upper-left corner of the window or dialog box, or press **Alt** and the **Spacebar**.

2 Click on a menu option, or press the selection letter.

GETTING HELP

What Is Help?

Help is exactly what it sounds like—assistance with some task you are trying to perform. Windows has a sophisticated on-line Help system that can display information on the screen about any Windows task.

Help information is displayed in a standard format and has certain features that assist you in finding the needed information. If you can't remember how to perform a particular task, you don't have to stop and look it up in the Windows User's Guide. Program Manager, File Manager, Print Manager, and many other Windows applications offer their own on-line help facility.

You can get help by using the Contents or Search buttons in the Help window to find help topics. Within a Help topic, there may also be one or more *jumps*, which you can click (or select and press **Enter**) to display a new Help topic. Jumps are links which you can click on (or select and press **Enter**) to display a new, but related, Help topic. A jump can be text or graphics, and when you move the mouse pointer over a jump, the mouse pointer changes shape (becomes a hand with the index finger pointing at the jump). To choose a jump, simply click on the topic once the pointer changes shape.

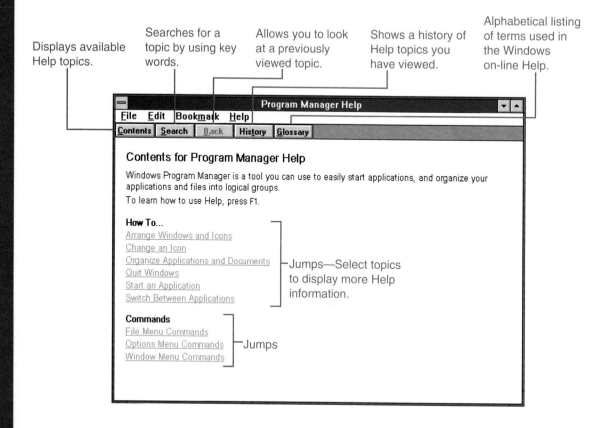

Using Help

1 Click on **Help** in the menu bar, or press **Alt+H**.

2 To display the Search dialog box, click on **S**earch for Help on, or press **S**.

3 Type the word or phrase for which you want to search. When you start typing, the words that most closely match the text you type are displayed in the list box.

4 Click the **S**how Topics button, or press **Alt+S**.

5 Click the **G**o To button, or press **Alt+G**. The topic will appear in a new Help Window.

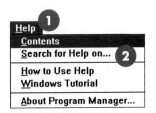

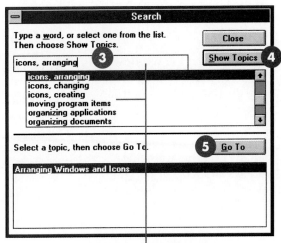

As you type the word or phrase for which you are searching, related topics appear in the list box.

LEARNING THE LINGO

Jumps: Links that you can click on (or select and press **Enter**) to display a Help topic.

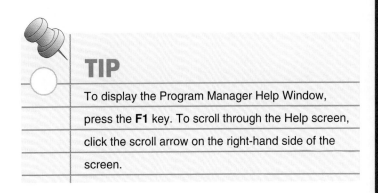

TIP

To display the Program Manager Help Window, press the **F1** key. To scroll through the Help screen, click the scroll arrow on the right-hand side of the screen.

Beginning Windows Tasks

GETTING HELP

Exercise

This exercise will show you how to use **Help** to find information on how to arrange Windows and Icons.

1 Display the **Help** menu, by clicking on **Help** in the menu bar, or pressing **Alt+H**.

2 Click on **Search** for Help, or press **S**.

3 In the text box, type **Windows**.

4 Select the **Show** Topics button, or press **Alt+S**.

5 Select the **Go** To button, or press **Alt+G**. The Arranging Windows and Icons topic will appear in a new Help Window.

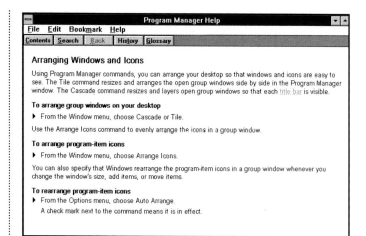

Program Manager Help

File   Edit   Bookmark   Help

Contents | Search | Back | History | Glossary

Arranging Windows and Icons

Using Program Manager commands, you can arrange your desktop so that windows and icons are easy to see. The Tile command resizes and arranges the open group windows side by side in the Program Manager window. The Cascade command resizes and layers open group windows so that each title bar is visible.

To arrange group windows on your desktop
▶ From the Window menu, choose Cascade or Tile.

Use the Arrange Icons command to evenly arrange the icons in a group window.

To arrange program-item icons
▶ From the Window menu, choose Arrange Icons.

You can also specify that Windows rearrange the program-item icons in a group window whenever you change the window's size, add items, or move items.

To rearrange program-item icons
▶ From the Options menu, choose Auto Arrange.
   A check mark next to the command means it is in effect.

EXITING WINDOWS

When to Exit Windows

When you finish a Windows session, you should exit the program and return to the DOS prompt before turning off the computer. This allows windows to save changes you have made to the Program Manager layout and to delete, from the hard disk, temporary files that windows routinely saves during your work sessions.

How to Exit Windows

1 Click on File, or press **Alt+F**.

2 Click on Exit Windows, or press **X**.

3 Click on the **OK** button, or press **Enter** in the Exit Windows Dialog box to confirm that you want to exit Windows and return to DOS.

TIP

To save the arrangement of Program Manager windows and icons so that the desktop will be arranged in the same manner the next time you start Windows, select Save Settings on Exit, from the **O**ptions menu before you exit Windows.

TIP

A shortcut way to exit Windows is to double-click the Control-menu box or press **Alt+F4**.

If you change your mind and do not want to end your Windows session, click on the **Cancel** button in the Exit Windows Dialog Box, or press **ESC**.

Beginning Windows Tasks

PART 2

Program Manager Essentials

The Program Manager is the foundation of Windows. When you start up Windows, the Program Manager automatically loads and is always running during your Windows session. You can use Program Manager to organize your applications, create new icons, and switch between programs.

- Running Applications
- Switching Between Group Windows
- Switching Between Applications
- Creating Program Groups
- Creating Program Item Icons
- Deleting Group and Application Icons

- Renaming Group and Application Icons
- Moving an Application Icon
- Examining the Contents of the Clipboard
- Changing Colors
- Changing Wallpaper

RUNNING APPLICATIONS

How to Run an Application

Windows is an operating environment that allows you to start up your programs and to manage your files. You can run many different types of applications under Windows. Programs have been written specifically for use with Windows, but other programs (called non-Windows applications) that have been designed for DOS, in many cases, can also run under Windows.

When you are ready to begin working with your programs, you can use Windows to run or start up an application. To do that you must first open the group window that contains the program you want to run. Group windows can contain both programs and files, which are represented by *icons*. For example, you can have a group window for all your Lotus programs, such as 1-2-3, Ami Pro, and Agenda.

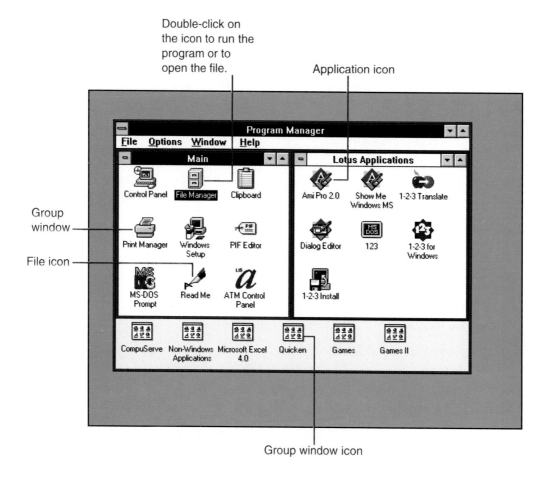

Double-click on the icon to run the program or to open the file.

Application icon

Group window

File icon

Group window icon

Running Applications

1 If the Program Manager window is not open, double-click on the **Program Manager** icon. If you are using the keyboard, press **Alt+Esc** repeatedly until you select the **Program Manager** icon, and press **Enter**.

2 Position the mouse pointer over the group window icon that contains the application icon and double-click on it (or if the group window is open, click anywhere on the window to make the window active). With the keyboard, press **Ctrl+Tab** until you select the group window, and then press **Enter**.

3 Double-click on the icon, or press the arrow keys until you select the icon of the application you want to run, and then press **Enter**. The application's window opens and the program is up and running.

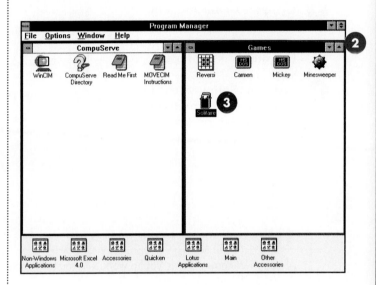

LEARNING THE LINGO

Active window: A window you are currently using or have selected. Only one window can be active at one time.

Application: A software program such as word processing, spreadsheet, or database.

Group: A collection of applications or documents within Program Manager.

Group icon: A small picture that represents a group of applications or documents in Program Manager.

Group window: A window that displays the items in a group within Program Manager.

Icon: A small picture that represents a program group, application, document, or other element of Windows.

Program Manager Essentials

RUNNING APPLICATIONS

Exercise

Let's have some fun! Practice running an application by running the Solitaire application that is contained in the Game Group.

1 If the Program Manager window is not open, open it by double-clicking on the icon or pressing **Alt+Esc**.

2 Open the **Game** group by double-clicking or selecting the group icon with the arrow keys and pressing **Enter**.

3 Select the **Solitaire** icon by double-clicking or selecting the icon with the arrow keys and pressing **Enter**.

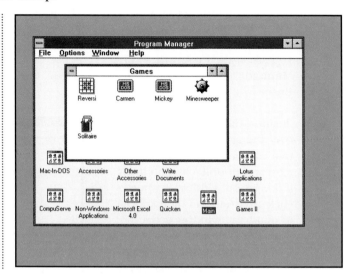

TIP

Although Windows allows you to work with multiple windows at a time, your screen can get cluttered and confusing with multiple open windows. Therefore, when you are finished with a window or the desktop is too cluttered, you can close a window by double-clicking on the window's **Control** menu or pressing **Ctrl+F4**.

SWITCHING BETWEEN GROUP WINDOWS

Why Switch Between Group Windows?

Windows 3.1 allows you to switch quickly between group windows so that you can run multiple applications. You can work on a spreadsheet, then switch to the group containing your word processing program, and you can run that program. To run another application or work with the files within another group window, you must make that group window *active*. A window is active when you *select* it. If you work with a mouse, the easiest way to switch between windows is to click on the window to which you want to switch. If you use the keyboard, you can switch between group windows by choosing a group name from the Window menu's list of groups.

To switch to another group window using the keyboard, press **ALT+W**, and press the number that corresponds to the name of the group to which you want to switch.

Use your mouse to click on the window to which you want to switch.

A check mark appears next to the active window.

List of group names.

Select a group name from the **W**indow menu to switch to that group window.

If the group you want to switch to is an icon, double-click on it.

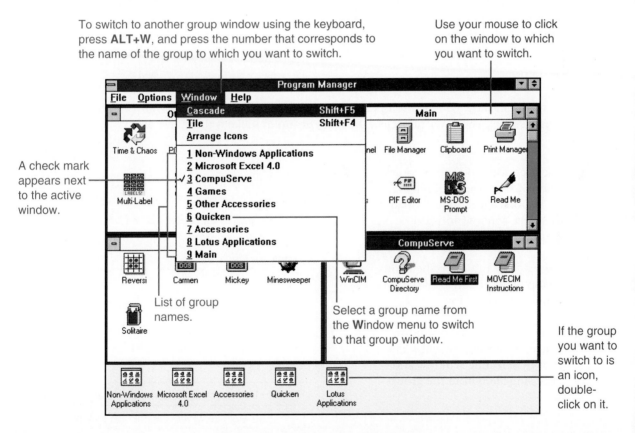

LEARNING THE LINGO

Active window: A window you are currently using or have selected. Only one window can be active at one time.

List of groups: The names of all the groups that are listed at the bottom of the **W**indow menu.

Program Manager Essentials

SWITCHING BETWEEN GROUP WINDOWS

Switching Between Windows

1 If the window is visible, click on any part of it to make it active or click on the Window menu in the menu bar, or press **Alt+W**. A list of numbered windows appears with the currently active window checked.

2 If you are using the **Window** menu, click on the name of the group window that you want to make active, or press the number corresponding to the group name. A check mark appears next to the activated window.

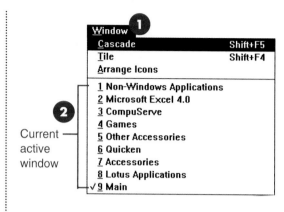

Current active window

Exercise

This exercise will show you how to open the Accessories, Main, and Game windows, respectively. Then you can select the Main group to make it the active window.

1 Use the mouse pointer to point to the Accessories group icon and double-click on it to open or select **Window** and choose Accessories from the group list.

2 Repeat step 1 to open the main group window and then the Game group window.

3 Make the Main group window active by clicking anywhere on it or by selecting **Window** and choosing Main from the group list.

TIP

There are two ways to tell if a window has been selected (active):

- The title bar of an active window is a different color or a stronger intensity of color than any other visible title bars.

- If the desktop has windows that overlap, then the active window is the one on top.

TIP

You can also select a group window by pressing **Ctrl+Tab** until the window or group icon of your choice becomes available.

SWITCHING BETWEEN APPLICATIONS

Why Switch Between Applications?

Once you have multiple applications running, you can quickly switch between those applications, without exiting from the application in which you are working. The capability to switch between open applications allows you to share data and move quickly from one task to another. For example, you may be using Windows' Calculator, which is an application in the Accessories group window, and, at the same time, you may have a word processing application open. You can use the Calculator to "crunch" some numbers and then switch back to the word processing document to input your calculated numbers.

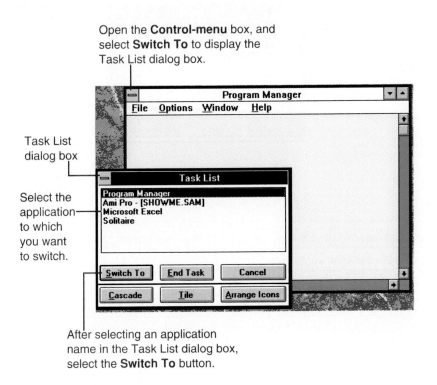

Open the **Control-menu** box, and select **Switch To** to display the Task List dialog box.

Task List dialog box

Select the application to which you want to switch.

After selecting an application name in the Task List dialog box, select the **Switch To** button.

SWITCHING BETWEEN APPLICATIONS

Switching Between Applications

1 Click on the **Control-menu** box, in the upper-left corner of the window, or press **Alt+Spacebar** to display the Control menu.

2 Click on Switch To, or press **W**.

3 Click on the name of the application to which you want to switch, or use the arrow keys to highlight the name of the application.

4 Click on the Switch To button, or press **Alt+S**.

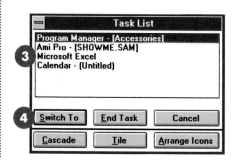

TIP

With the Task List displayed, you can double-click on the name of an application to switch to it. There are a few other ways to switch between applications:

- Press **Alt+Esc** until the window you want is active.
- Press and hold down **Alt** while pressing **Tab** repeatedly to cycle through running applications.
- Press **Ctrl+Esc** or double-click anywhere on the desktop to open the Task List.
- Double-click anywhere on the Windows desktop (except on a window) to display the Task List dialog box, then double-click on the name of the application to which you want to switch. You can also click on any visible application window or application icon to make it active.

CREATING PROGRAM GROUPS

Why Create Program Groups?

Program groups are a collection of applications and files within the Program Manager. Windows uses groups as a way to organize your program items. You can add new groups to your Program Manager any time you have the need to reorganize your desktop. For example, if you have a collection of programs that are similar but are located in several groups, you can create a new group and move the application icons into that new group. You must create program groups before you can add program items to the group.

To add a new group, you use the **File New** command to display the New Program Object dialog box.

Select to add a new group.

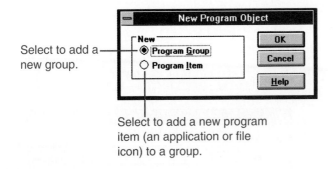

Select to add a new program item (an application or file icon) to a group.

Creating Program Groups

➊ Click on **File**, or press **Alt+F** in the menu bar of the Program Manager.

➋ Click on **New**, or press **N**.

➌ Click on the Program Group option button, or press **G**.

➍ Click on **OK**, or press **Enter**.

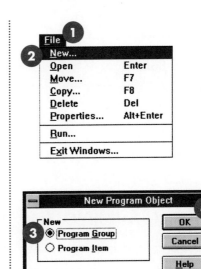

35

CREATING PROGRAM GROUPS

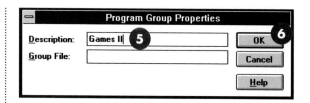

5 In the Description text box, type a description of the group you want to create. This description will appear in the title box of the group window and below the group icon. Therefore, give some thought to how you want to describe the group before entering a description.

6 Click on the **OK** button, or press **Enter**. The new group will be added to Program Manager.

Exercise

Try your hand at adding a new program group. Create a new group named Games II.

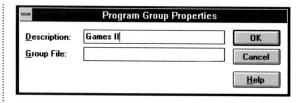

1 Click on **File**, or press **Alt+F**.

2 Click on **New** or press **N**.

3 Click on the Program **G**roup option button, or press **G**.

4 Click on **OK**, or press **Enter**.

5 In the **D**escription text box, type New Group.

6 Click on the **OK** button, or press **Enter**. The New Group will be added to Program Manager.

LEARNING THE LINGO

Program group: A collection of applications and files that are displayed as icons in a window.

Program item: An application or file, as represented by an icon, in a program group.

CREATING PROGRAM ITEM ICONS

Why Create Program Item Icons?

Program-item icons represent applications or files that can be run by an application. For example, the Write icon represents the program file named WRITE.EXE, which is the Write word processing program. You can create a document using Write and create a program-item icon for that document file. That way, you can open Write and the document together by selecting its icon from a group window.

If you work with a document or other file often, it may be more efficient for you to create a program-item icon and place that icon in a group window so that when you want to open the file, you select or double-click on the icon.

To create a program-item, you select **File New** to display the New Program Object dialog box. Once you select the New Program **I**tem option button, Windows displays the Program Items Properties box into which you enter information that tells Windows facts about the file, which are called the program item's properties. After a program item has been created, you can go back and change any of its properties.

Select the Program Item option button to add a program item to a group.

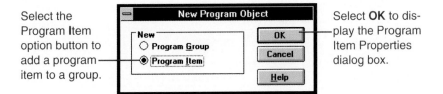

Select **OK** to display the Program Item Properties dialog box.

<table>
<tr><td colspan="2" align="center">New Program Object</td><td></td></tr>
<tr><td colspan="2">New</td><td>OK</td></tr>
<tr><td>○</td><td>Program **G**roup</td><td>Cancel</td></tr>
<tr><td>◉</td><td>Program **I**tem</td><td>**H**elp</td></tr>
</table>

Program Manager Essentials

CREATING PROGRAM ITEM ICONS

(Optional) Directory where the application's files are located. If blank, Windows uses the directory where the application's files are located.

A description of the program-item icon

Select **B**rowse to search for the file name and directory.

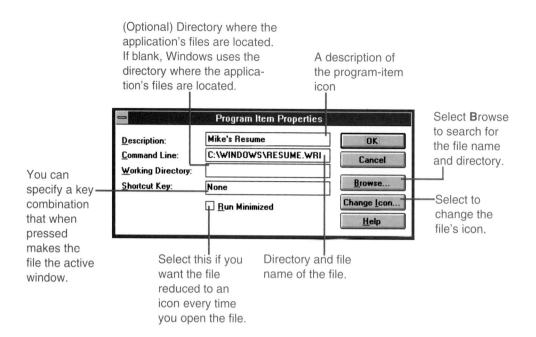

You can specify a key combination that when pressed makes the file the active window.

Select this if you want the file reduced to an icon every time you open the file.

Directory and file name of the file.

Select to change the file's icon.

TIP

You can also create a program item by using a mouse to drag a program or document file from File Manager to a Program Manager group. The Windows File Manager is reviewed in Part 3 of this book.

TIP

Instead of entering the **C**ommand Line information in the Program Item Properties text box, select the **B**rowse button, or press **Alt+B** to display the Browse dialog box that allows you to search your directories for the file name to associate with the program-item icon.

Creating Program Item Icons

1 Open the group window that you want to add an item to by double-clicking on its icon or pressing **Alt+W**.

2 Select the group by clicking on the group name or typing the corresponding number.

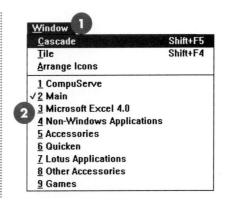

3 Click on **File**, or press **Alt+F**.

4 Click on **New**, or press **N**.

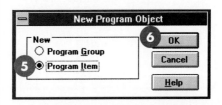

5 In the New Program Object dialog box, click on the Program Item option button, or press **I**.

6 Click on the **OK** button, or press **Enter**.

7 In the **D**escription text box, enter the file's description.

8 In the **C**ommand Line text box, enter the directory and file name (path) of the file you want to associate with the program-item icon.

9 Click on the **OK** button, or press **Enter**.

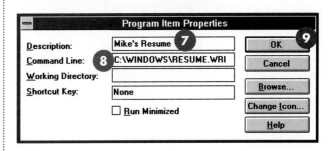

Program Manager Essentials

DELETING GROUP AND APPLICATION ICONS

Why Delete Icons?

There will be times when you will want to delete a group or application from your Program Manager. You may find that some groupings of applications and files no longer meet your needs or that the files within the group are obsolete. You may also want to remove some applications and files from your hard disk to free up space.

To delete a group icon, you must first reduce (minimize) the window of the group to an icon. Then you can select the icon and use the **File Delete** command.

With the group icon selected, use the **F**ile **D**elete command to delete the group.

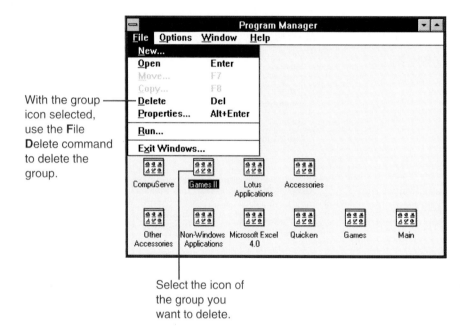

Select the icon of the group you want to delete.

LEARNING THE LINGO

Control-menu: Menu of commands to manipulate windows, dialog boxes, and icons (that is, restore, move, size, and close).

Deleting Icons

1 Select the icon you want to delete by clicking on it. If you are using the keyboard and you want to delete a group, press **Ctrl+Tab** until you select the group window, and then press **Enter**. If you are deleting an application icon, use the arrow keys to move from icon to icon until you select the one to be deleted.

2 Click on the **File** menu, and then click on **Delete**. If you are using the keyboard, press the **Del** key.

3 Click on the **Yes** button, or press **Enter**.

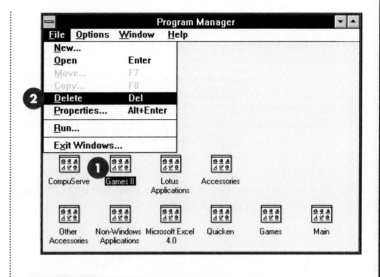

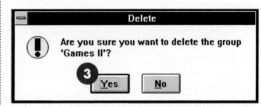

QUICK REFRESHER

To open a group window's Control menu so that you can minimize it to an icon, click the Control box in the upper-left corner of the window. If you are using the keyboard, press **Alt** and the **Spacebar**.

Program Manager Essentials

RENAMING GROUP AND APPLICATION ICONS

Why Rename an Icon?

When you create an icon, you name the icon by entering a description in the Program Item Properties dialog box. An icon's name and description are synonymous. You may find that your description needs revising because the nature of the group or file has changed in some way. The command **File Properties** allows you to change the properties of a program item or group. The command line (path), working directory, and program-item icon are all properties of a file. The dialog box that appears when you choose **Properties** depends on what you select. If you select a program item, the Program Item Properties dialog box appears. If you select a group, the Program Group Properties dialog box appears.

To change the
icon's name, enter
a new description.

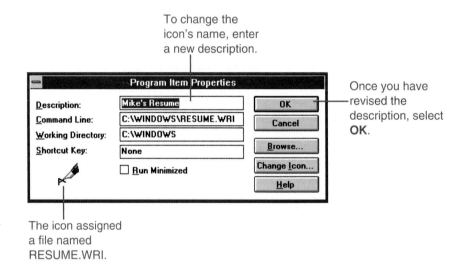

Once you have
revised the
description, select
OK.

The icon assigned
a file named
RESUME.WRI.

LEARNING THE LINGO

File properties: The command line (path), working directory, and program-item icon associated with a particular file.

42

Renaming Group and Application Icons

1 Click on the group or application icon you want to rename. If you are using the keyboard, and you want to rename a group icon, press **Ctrl+Tab** until you select the group window, and then press **Enter**. If you are renaming an application icon, use the arrow keys to move from icon to icon until you select the one to rename.

2 Click on the File menu, or press **Alt+F**.

3 Click on Properties, or press **P**.

4 In the Description text box, enter the new description.

5 Click on **OK**, or press **Enter**.

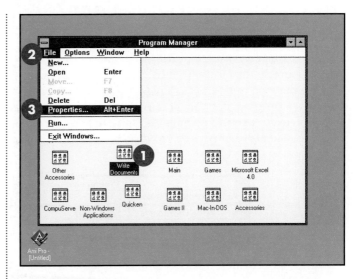

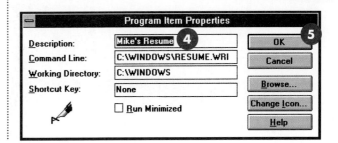

TIP
You can use the **File Properties** command to change any one of the properties of an icon, including the command line (path) and working directory, and, in some cases, the appearance of the icon.

Program Manager Essentials

MOVING AN APPLICATION ICON

Why Move an Application Icon?

As you work in Windows, you may find better ways to organize your group windows. This may involve moving application icons from one window to another. You can use the mouse to move icons from one window to another. You simply drag the icon out of its current window to the new group window. When you move a program item, it is removed from its original group. If you are using the keyboard to execute commands, you can select the icon to be moved and then select **File Move** or press F7 to display the Move Program Item dialog box.

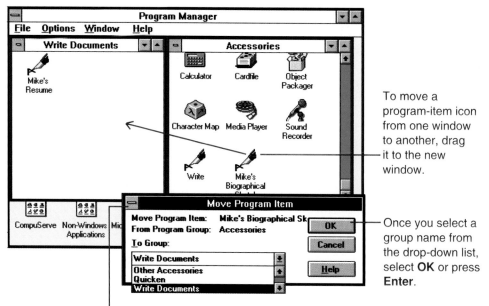

To move a program-item icon from one window to another, drag it to the new window.

Once you select a group name from the drop-down list, select **OK** or press **Enter**.

Press **F7** to display the Move Program Item dialog box, and use the down arrow keys to cycle through the group names in the **To** Group drop-down box.

LEARNING THE LINGO

Drag: Point to an item, and then press and hold the mouse button as you move the mouse, dragging the item around the display. When finished dragging, release the mouse button.

Program item: An application or file as represented by an icon in a program group.

Moving an Application Icon

1 Open the group window that contains the program item you want to move.

2 Open the destination-group window, or leave the destination group as an icon, if you don't care where the icon for the moved item is placed in the group.

3 Drag the program-item icon to the destination-group icon or window. If you are using a keyboard, press **F7** to display the Move Program Item dialog box, and use the up and down arrow keys to cycle through the list of group names.

4 Release the mouse button when the icon is on top of the destination-group window or icon. If you are using the keyboard, press **Enter** to place the icon in the destination window.

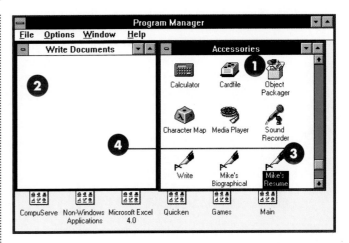

QUICK REFRESHER

To open a group window:

1. Click on **W**indow in the menu bar, or press **Alt+W**. A list of numbered windows appears with the currently active window checked.

2. Click on the name of the group window that you want to open, or press the number that corresponds with the name of the group to which you want to switch.

You can also open a group window by double-clicking on its icon or by pressing **Ctrl+Tab** until you select the icon and then press **Enter** to open it.

Program Manager Essentials

MOVING AN APPLICATION ICON

Exercise

For practice, let's move the Character Map icon in the Accessories group to the Main group and then move it back to the Accessories group.

1 Open the group window that contains the program item you want to move.

2 Open the destination-group window, or leave the destination group as an icon, if you don't care where the icon for the moved item is placed.

3 Move the icon by either dragging it or pressing **F7** and using the Move Program Item dialog box to accomplish the move.

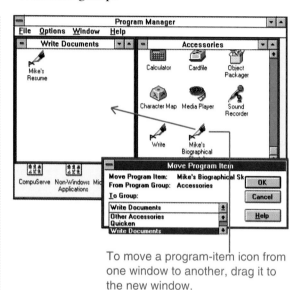

To move a program-item icon from one window to another, drag it to the new window.

EXAMINING THE CONTENTS OF THE CLIPBOARD

Why Examine the Clipboard?

The Windows' Clipboard is a temporary storage area that helps you transfer information between documents and applications. When you cut or copy information from an application, the information is temporarily stored on the Clipboard. You then paste that information from the Clipboard into other documents or applications. You can see what is stored on the Clipboard by using Clipboard Viewer. The Clipboard Viewer icon is in the Main group.

You can view, delete, and save the contents of the Clipboard. By saving the Clipboard contents, you can paste them into a document at a later time.

Select the Display menu to change the format of the contents

Contents of Clipboard

Text that has been copied or cut from a document or application.

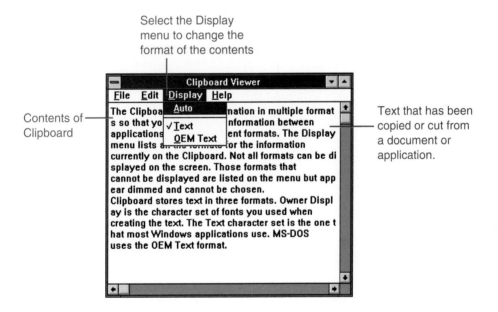

LEARNING THE LINGO

Clipboard: An application that acts as a temporary storage area and can be used to transfer data between documents and applications.

Paste: To copy the contents of the Clipboard to a document or application.

EXAMINING THE CONTENTS OF THE CLIPBOARD

Examining the Contents of the Clipboard

1 Open the **Main** group window by clicking on the **Window** menu or pressing **Alt+F**.

2 Click on **Main**, or press the corresponding number.

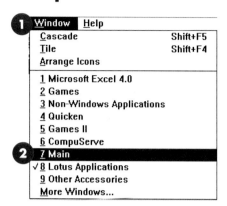

3 Double-click on the **Clipboard Viewer** icon. If you are using the keyboard, press the right or left arrow keys until you select the **Clipboard Viewer** icon, and then press **Enter**.

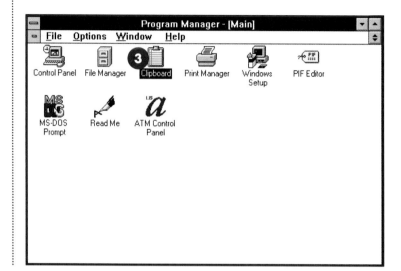

QUICK REFRESHER

To open a group window, double-click on the icon or press **Ctrl+Tab** until you select one window, then press **Enter** to open it. You can also open a group window by selecting **W**indow and choosing the group from the list.

Exercise

Open the Accessories Group and press the **Print Screen** key to capture a picture
of your desktop, which will be placed on the Clipboard.

1 Open the **Accessories** group
window.

2 Press the **Print Screen** key.

3 Open the **Main** group window.

4 To see the contents of the
Clipboard, double-click on the
Clipboard Viewer icon. If you
are using the keyboard, press
the right or left arrow keys
until you select the **Clipboard
Viewer** icon, and then press
Enter.

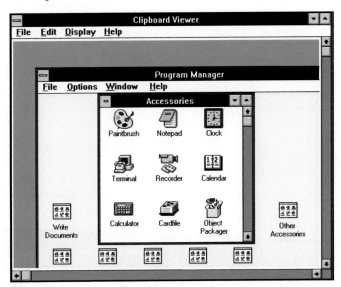

Program Manager Essentials

CHANGING COLORS

Why Change Colors?

You can change the way Windows looks by changing the colors. You can have fun changing the colors to fit your mood, or you can select colors to reduce eyestrain. Windows comes with several predefined color schemes from which you can choose, or you can create custom colors.

To change screen colors, you use the Colors option of the Control Panel. Control Panel is a Windows application that provides a visual way of modifying your system while working with Windows.

The Color Schemes drop-down list includes several predefined color schemes.

You can modify a color scheme by changing the color of screen elements and then saving your changes.

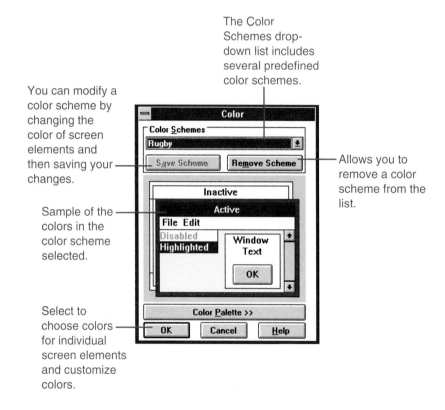

Allows you to remove a color scheme from the list.

Sample of the colors in the color scheme selected.

Select to choose colors for individual screen elements and customize colors.

Changing Colors

1 Click on **Window**, or press **Alt+W**.

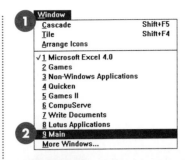

2 Click on **Main**, or press the corresponding number.

3 Double-click on the **Control Panel** icon, or use the arrow keys to select the **Control Panel** icon, and press **Enter**.

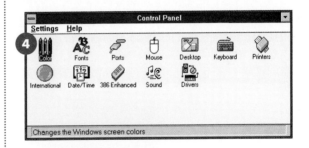

4 Double-click on the **Color** icon, or use the arrow keys to select the **Color** icon, and press **Enter**.

5 Open the Color **S**chemes list, by clicking on its down arrow and clicking on a color scheme. If you are using the keyboard, use the up and down arrows to select a color scheme. As you cycle through the color scheme names, the colors of the elements in the sample screen change to reflect the scheme you select.

6 Click on the **OK** button, or press **Enter**.

Program Manager Essentials

CHANGING COLORS

Exercise

To practice changing Windows' colors, let's change the color scheme to Ocean.

1 Open the **Main** group.

2 Select the **Control Panel** icon.

3 Select the **Color** icon.

4 Open the Color **S**chemes list, and select **Ocean**.

5 Select the **OK** button, or press **Enter**.

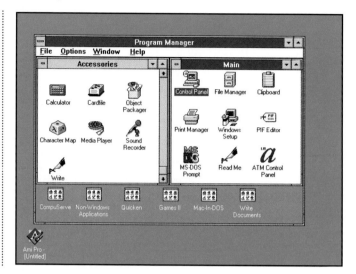

LEARNING THE LINGO

Color schemes: A combination of colors of screen elements.

Screen elements: Parts that make up a window or dialog box such as the title bars, borders, and scroll bars of a window or dialog box.

CHANGING WALLPAPER

Why Change the Wallpaper?

Wallpaper is an image that is displayed on the desktop background. There are several different wallpaper patterns that are available in Windows. You can try different wallpapers to determine which one you find the most appealing and fun. Each different type of wallpaper is a *bitmap*, which is a graphical image stored in a file and made up of a pattern of dots.

Not only can you change from one wallpaper pattern to another, you can use bitmap files created by Paintbrush or any other painting application. To change a wallpaper pattern, you use the Desktop application found in the Control Panel.

Select the Screen Saver Name from the list to display an animated screen during times of inactivity.

Displays a list of bitmap files that can be used as Wallpaper.

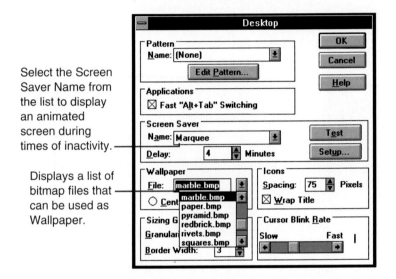

LEARNING THE LINGO

Bitmap: A graphical image stored in a file and made up of a pattern of dots.

Paintbrush: A drawing program found in the Accessories group.

Wallpaper: An image that is displayed on the desktop background.

Program Manager Essentials

CHANGING WALLPAPER

Changing Wallpaper

1 Click on Window, or press **Alt+W**.

2 Click on **Main**, or enter the corresponding number.

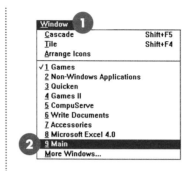

3 Double-click on the **Control Panel** icon, or use the arrow keys to select the **Control Panel** icon, and press **Enter**.

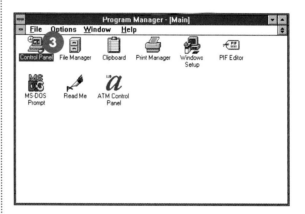

4 Double-click on the **Desktop** icon, or use the arrow keys to select the **Desktop** icon, and press **Enter**.

5 Under the Wallpaper section of the Desktop dialog box, open the **File** list by clicking on its down arrow, and then select the wallpaper file you want to use. If you are using the keyboard, press **Alt+F**, and then use the down arrow key to cycle through the list of wallpaper files.

6 You can click on the **Center** or **Tile** option buttons, or press **Alt+C** or **Alt+T** to position the wallpaper on your screen.

7 Click on **OK**, or press **Enter**.

Exercise

For practice, let's change the Windows Wallpaper to the marble pattern.

1 Open the **Main** group window.

2 Select the **Control Panel** icon.

3 Select the **Desktop** icon.

4 Under the Wallpaper section of the Desktop dialog box, open the **File** list, and then select the MARBLE.BMP wallpaper file.

5 Select the **Tile** option button to repeat the wallpaper as many times as necessary to cover the entire screen.

6 Press **Enter** or click on **OK**.

```
Window   Help
  Cascade                    Shift+F5
  Tile                       Shift+F4
  Arrange Icons
  1 Microsoft Excel 4.0
  2 Games
  3 Non-Windows Applications
  4 Quicken
  5 Games II
  6 CompuServe
  7 Main
√ 8 Lotus Applications
  9 Other Accessories
  More Windows...
```

TIP

Select **C**enter to position the wallpaper in the center of your screen. Select **T**ile (if it is not already selected) to repeat the wallpaper as many times as necessary to cover the entire screen—much like a tiled floor. If you are using the keyboard, press **Alt+C** (for Center) or **Alt+T** (Tile).

TIP

You can also use the Desktop dialog box to select a Screen Saver. A *Screen Saver* is an animated display that automatically appears on your screen when you don't use the keyboard or the mouse for a specified period of time. If you select the Screen Saver Name drop-down list, you can choose from a list of several screen savers. Then you can enter, in the Delay box, the number of minutes of inactivity necessary to trigger the display of the Screen Saver.

Program Manager Essentials

PART 3

File Manager

The File Manager is a powerful application found within the Main group. You can use it to manage disks, directories, and files. From within File Manager, you can view the structure of your disks and see what your directories contain. You can also use the File Manager to format your floppy disks and to copy and move your files from one drive or directory to another. The twelve tasks of this part of the book show you the basics of the File Manager.

- Opening and Closing File Manager
- Selecting a Drive
- Selecting a Directory
- Expanding and Collapsing a Directory
- Examining a Directory's File List
- Creating and Naming Directories
- Selecting Multiple Files
- Renaming Files
- Copying Files
- Opening Another Directory Window
- Moving Files
- Searching for a File
- Formatting a Disk

OPENING AND CLOSING FILE MANAGER

Why Open and Close File Manager?

You can use File Manager to organize and manage your files and directories. With File Manager, you can move and copy files, start applications, and format disks. Before you can use File Manager, you must first open it. File Manager can be found in the Main group window. As is the case with any application with which you work, when you are through working with File Manager you should close it.

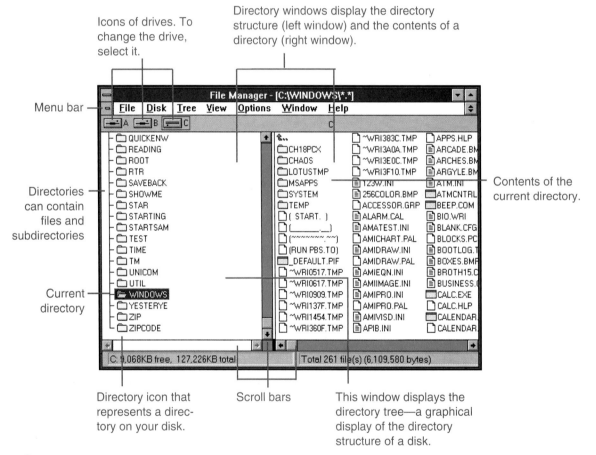

Icons of drives. To change the drive, select it.

Directory windows display the directory structure (left window) and the contents of a directory (right window).

Menu bar

Directories can contain files and subdirectories

Current directory

Contents of the current directory.

Directory icon that represents a directory on your disk.

Scroll bars

This window displays the directory tree—a graphical display of the directory structure of a disk.

TIP

You can also close the File Manager by double-clicking on its Control-menu box.

Opening and Closing File Manager

1 If the Program Manager window is not open, double-click its icon to open it, or press **Alt+Esc** repeatedly until you select the Program Manager icon, and press **Enter**.

2 If the Main group is not the active window, click on it to select it or press **Ctrl+Tab** until you select it. You can also click on **Window** or press **Alt+F** and select main.

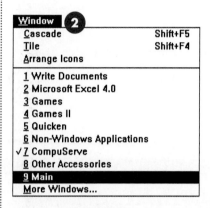

3 Double-click the **File Manager** icon, or press the arrow keys until you select the File Manager, and then press **Enter**.

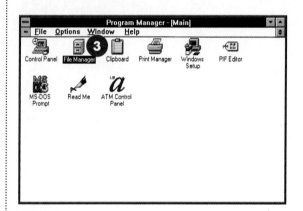

4 Once you are finished working with the File Manager, click on the File menu, or press **Alt+F**.

5 Click on Exit, or press **X**.

SELECTING A DRIVE

Why Select a Drive?

Above the left directory window in File Manager are icons for each drive for which you currently have access. The directories and files for the current drive are displayed in the two windows of the File Manager. The window on the left side of the screen shows the directories found on the disk in the current drive while the right window displays subdirectories and files.

You select a drive based on what you need to do with File Manager. For example, if you need to view the files of a disk that is in drive B of your computer, you would select the B drive icon. If you want to display the contents of a different disk, you select a different drive.

Drive B has been selected. To select a drive, click its icon or press Ctrl + the letter of the drive.

The contents of the disk in the selected drive (B) are shown in this window.

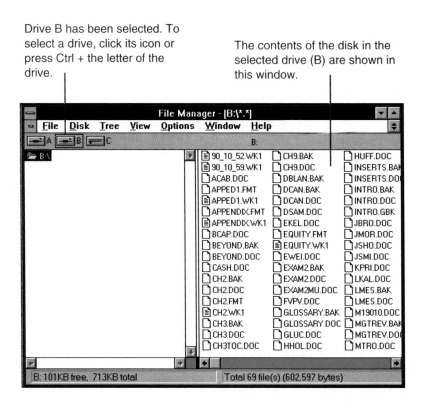

LEARNING THE LINGO

Directory: The structure of a disk; the way that disks are divided up. Directories contain files and other directories called subdirectories.

Drive: A device for saving and retrieving information on disk. A drive reads from and writes to a disk.

Subdirectory: A directory within a directory.

Selecting a Drive

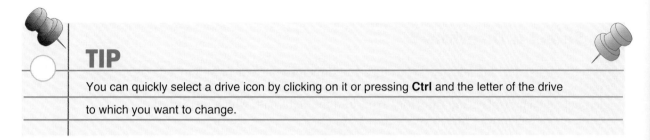

TIP

You can quickly select a drive icon by clicking on it or pressing **Ctrl** and the letter of the drive to which you want to change.

1 Click on the **D**isk menu, or press **Alt+D**.

2 Click on **S**elect Drive, or press **S**.

3 Select the drive by clicking on it or by using the arrow keys.

4 Click on **OK**, or press **Enter**.

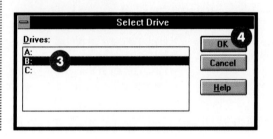

File Manager

SELECTING A DIRECTORY

Why Select a Directory?

When you use the File Manager, your files and directories are displayed in a directory window. The two windows that make up the directory window include: the left half, which displays the Directory Tree, and the right half, which displays the contents of the current directory.

You must select the directory that you want to view. As you select different directories in the Directory Tree, the contents of that directory are displayed in the right half of the window.

In the directory window, each file name has its own icon. An icon is a small picture that represents some element of windows, such as a file or application. To select a directory using the mouse, you click on the icon. To select a directory using the keyboard, use the arrow keys to highlight the directory.

The title bar shows the name of the selected directory.

Use the vertical scroll bar to view other directory names in the Directory Tree.

The subdirectories and files of the selected directory are displayed in this window.

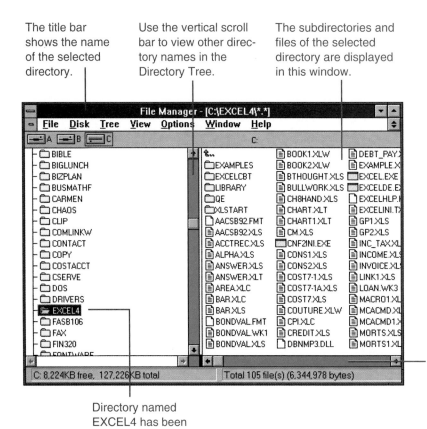

Directory named EXCEL4 has been selected.

Use the horizontal scroll bars to view the names of other files in the selected directory.

Selecting a Directory

1 Click a directory icon in the Directory Tree (the left side of the directory window) or press **Tab** to move to the Directory Tree, and then use the up or down arrow keys to select a directory.

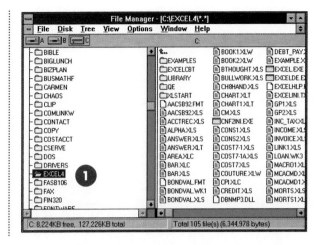

TIP

To quickly change to the root directory, press the **HOME** key, if you have the Directory Tree highlighted.

Exercise

To practice selecting directories, select the DOS directory from the Directory Tree.

1 Open the File Manager in the **Main** Group by double-clicking its icon or by using the arrow keys to select the File Manager icon and then press **Enter**.

2 Select the DOS directory in the left part of the directory window by clicking on the directory icon for DOS or by pressing **Tab** to move to the Directory Tree and then pressing the down arrow key to select DOS.

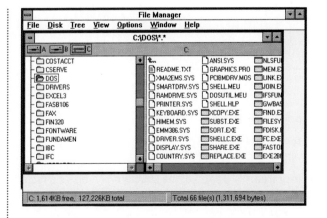

File Manager

EXPANDING AND COLLAPSING A DIRECTORY

Why Expand and Collapse a Directory?

Subdirectories are directories within a directory. For example, you might have a directory named BUDGETS and two subdirectories named BUDGET92 and BUDGET93 within the BUDGETS directory. If the directory you want to view is a subdirectory and does not appear in the Directory Tree, you can expand the directory so that you can see subdirectories. Once you have been able to view the expanded Directory Tree, you can collapse or hide the subdirectories so that you can view more of the directories on each screen.

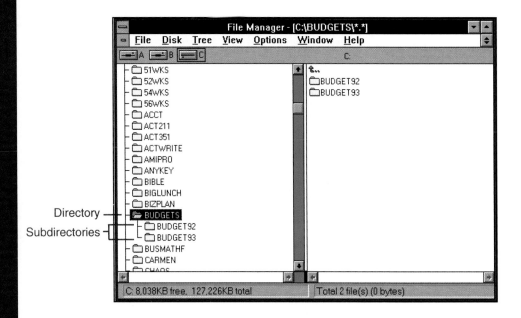

LEARNING THE LINGO

Collapsing a directory: To hide additional subdirectory levels below a directory in a directory tree.

Directory: The structure of a disk. The way in which disks are divided up. Directories contain files and other directories call subdirectories.

Directory tree: A display of the structure of a disk's directories with subdirectories represented as branches from a directory.

Expanding a directory: To show hidden subdirectory levels in a directory tree.

Subdirectory: A directory within a directory.

Expanding and Collapsing a Directory

1 Double-click the directory you want to expand in the Directory Tree (left side of the window), or select the directory by using the up or down arrow keys and pressing **Enter**.

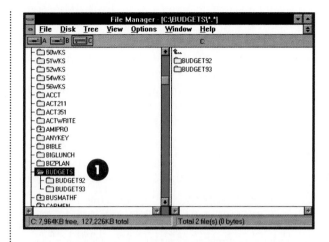

2 To collapse the directory, double-click the directory you want to collapse or select the directory by using the up or down arrow keys and pressing **Enter**.

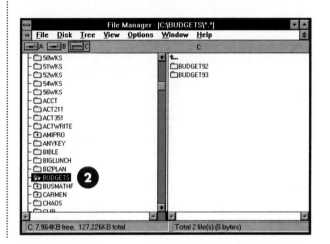

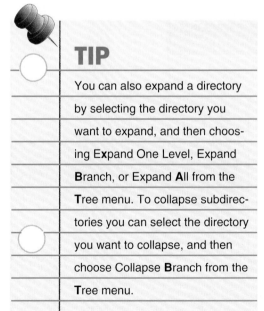

TIP

You can also expand a directory by selecting the directory you want to expand, and then choosing E**x**pand One Level, Expand **B**ranch, or Expand **A**ll from the **T**ree menu. To collapse subdirectories you can select the directory you want to collapse, and then choose Collapse **B**ranch from the **T**ree menu.

TIP

You can mark directories that have subdirectories by using the **I**ndicate Expandable Branches command on the **T**ree menu. A plus sign (+) will appear inside the directory icon (file folder) of all directories that have subdirectories.

File Manager

EXAMINING A DIRECTORY'S FILE LIST

Why Examine a Directory's File List?

When you first start File Manager, the left half of the directory window shows the Directory Tree, and the right half shows the names of all the files and directories in the selected (current) directory. You may want to view the list of files to determine which files to delete, which ones to move to another directory, or which ones you want to copy. If a directory has many files, you may not be able to see all of its files in the right half of the directory window. However, you can change the view of the directory window to see more files at one time. You can do this by choosing Directory **O**nly from the **V**iew menu.

Only the files of the selected directory are displayed when you choose View Directory Only.

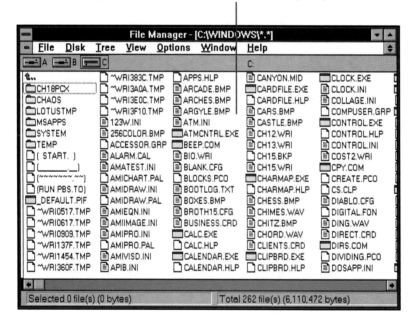

Check mark indicates current section.

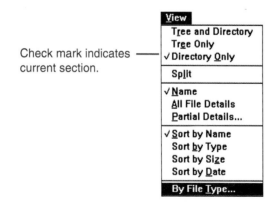

- **Tree and Directory**   Displays both the Directory Tree and the contents of the current directory in the directory window.

- **Tree Only**   Shows only the Directory Tree in the directory window.

- **Directory Only**   Displays only the contents (files and subdirectories) of the current directory window.

- **Split**   Moves the split bar left or right so that you can re-size the right and left parts of the directory window.

- **Name**   Displays only the names of files and directories in the directory window.

- **All File Details**   Displays all available information about files and directories in the active directory window, including the name, size, last modification date and time, and file attributes for each file.

- **Partial Details**   Displays specific file and directory information in the directory window with options including size, last modification date and time, and file attributes.

- **Sort by Name**   Sorts files alphabetically by file name.

- **Sort by Type**   Sorts files alphabetically by extension, then by filename.

- **Sort by Size**   Sorts files from largest to smallest.

- **Sort by Date**   Sorts files by last modification date, with the most recently modified file listed first.

- **By File Type**   Displays a group of files. You can choose to display directories, applications, or files with similar names.

LEARNING THE LINGO

Attributes: Information that indicates the type of file, such as a read-only, hidden, system or backup file.

Modification Time & Date: The last time and date the file was changed and saved.

Split bar: A dividing line that separates the left and right parts of the directory window. It can be moved to make one side larger and therefore display more information.

File Manager

Examining a Directory's File List

1 Click on the View menu, or press **Alt+V**.

2 Click on Directory **O**nly or press **O**.

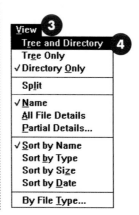

3 To go back to the split display showing both the Directory Tree and the files, click on the View menu, or press **Alt+V**.

4 Click on T**r**ee and Directory, or press **R**.

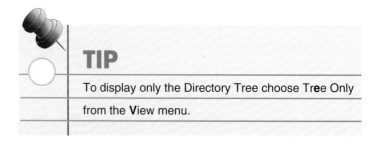

TIP

You can change the way Windows displays directories and files, the information that will be displayed and the way in which the files will be sorted before they are displayed in the directory window by selecting **V**iew and then choosing one or more of the twelve **V**iew menu choices.

TIP

To display only the Directory Tree choose T**r**ee Only from the **V**iew menu.

CREATING AND NAMING DIRECTORIES

Why Create and Name Directories?

Directories help you organize your files. Creating a directory is like setting up a file folder in a filing cabinet. Just as you may store certain letters and reports in a particular file folder, you can store certain files in a directory. Once you have created a directory, you can copy files and directories to it and save files to it using your application and programs.

To create a directory, you first select the directory within which you want the new directory. To make the new directory a branch (subdirectory) of the root directory, select **C:** in the Directory Tree (the left part of the directory window).

If you want the new directory
to be in the root directory,
select the icon for C:\.

If you want the
new directory to
be a subdirectory,
select that direc-
tory.

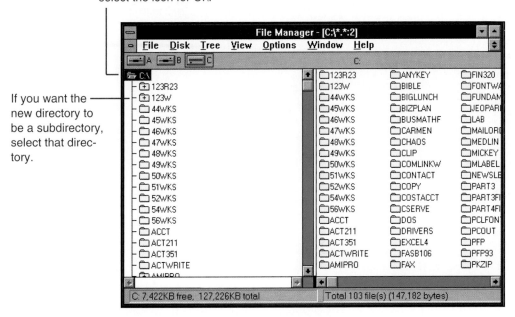

LEARNING THE
LINGO

Root directory: The top level
directory of a disk.

TIP

The directory name you assign should be descrip-

tive, contain up to eight characters, and start with

either a letter or number. Also, the directory name

cannot contain spaces. A directory name normally

does not include an extension.

CREATING AND NAMING DIRECTORIES

Creating and Naming Directories

1 Select the directory in which you want to create the new directory.

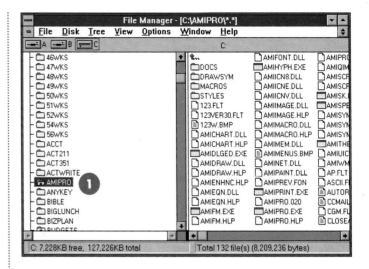

2 Click on the File menu, or press **Alt+F**.

3 Click on Create Directory, or press **E**.

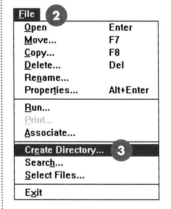

4 In the Create Directory dialog box, type the name of the new directory.

5 Click on the **OK** button, or press **Enter**.

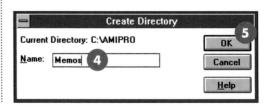

Exercise

To practice creating directories, create a directory named **NEW** that will be a sub-directory of your hard disk root directory.

1 Select the root directory (**C:**) by clicking on the C:\director icon or by pressing the up arrow key until it is highlighted.

2 Select the **F**ile menu by clicking it or by pressing **Alt+F**.

3 Choose C**r**eate Directory by clicking or pressing **E**.

4 In the Create Directory dialog box, type **NEW**.

5 Click on the **OK** button, or press **Enter**.

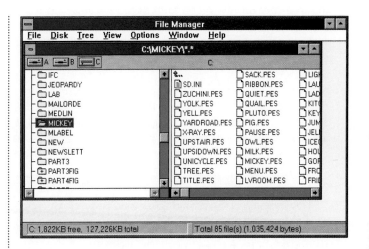

File Manager

SELECTING MULTIPLE FILES

Why Select Multiple Files?

You may want to select more than one file at a time to perform a task. For example, you may need to copy several files in a directory. Rather than copy one file at a time, you could select a group of files and copy them all one at a time. By selecting multiple files, you can then execute your command in one quick action. So if you want to delete a group of files, select them then delete them. Or maybe you want to move several files from one directory to another. You can select them then move them.

As with other Windows tasks, it is easier to select a group of files using the mouse. If the files are all in sequence, then you can select a group by clicking the first file and then clicking the remaining files while holding down the **Ctrl** key. If the files are out of sequence, hold down the **Ctrl** key as you select each file.

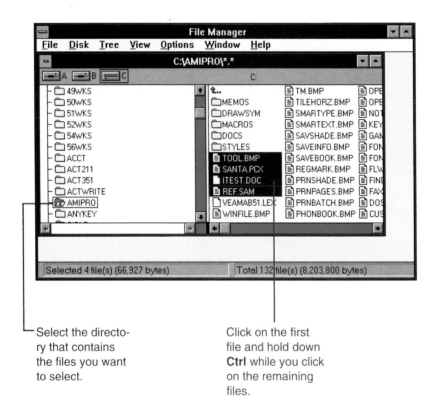

Select the directory that contains the files you want to select.

Click on the first file and hold down **Ctrl** while you click on the remaining files.

72

Selecting Multiple Files

1 Select the directory that contains the files you want to select by clicking the directories icon or by pressing the up and down arrow keys until you highlight the directory.

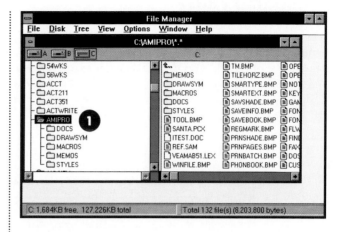

2 Click on the first file you want to select or press **Tab** and then the up or down arrow keys to highlight the first file.

3 Press and hold down **Shift** while you click the last file or directory in the group or use the up or down arrow keys to select the last file.

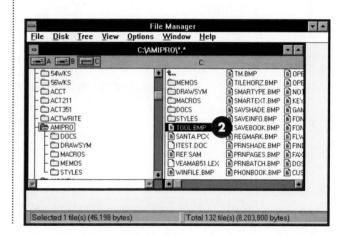

TIP

To select two or more files out of sequence press and hold down **Ctrl** while you click each file or directory. To select two or more files out of sequence using your keyboard:

1. Use the arrow keys to move to the first file you want to select.

2. Press and release **Shift+F8**. The selection cursor begins to blink.

3. Move to the next file you want to select.

4. Press the **Spacebar** to select each file.

5. Press **Shift+F8** when you finish selecting files.

File Manager

RENAMING FILES

Why Rename Files?

You may have a need to rename an existing file. For example, you may have a file named BUDGET.WK1 and you want to rename it BUDGET93.WK1 to be more descriptive of the file's contents. You can easily rename files using File Manager's **File Rename** command.

Select the file that you want to rename.

Select the directory that contains the file that you want to rename.

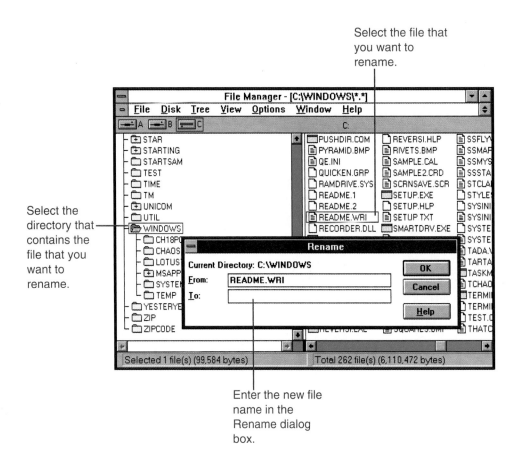

Enter the new file name in the Rename dialog box.

Renaming Files

1 Select the directory that contains the file you want to rename by clicking its directory icon or by pressing the up or down arrow keys until you highlight it.

2 Select the file you want to rename by clicking on it in the right part of the Directories window or by pressing TAB until you select the first file in the right part of the Directories window. Then use the arrow keys to select the file.

3 Click on the File menu, or press **Alt+F**.

4 Click on Rename, or press **N**.

5 In the Rename dialog box, type the new name.

6 Click on the **OK** button, or press **Enter**.

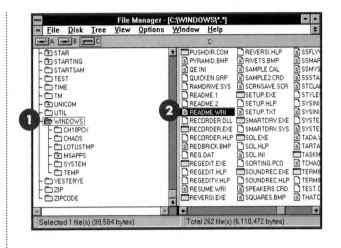

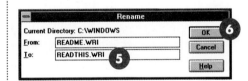

QUICK REFRESHER

To select a directory, click a directory icon in the Directory Tree (the left side of the directory window). If you are using the keyboard, press **Tab** to move to the Directory Tree, and then use the up or down arrow keys to select a directory.

File Manager

COPYING FILES

Why Copy Files?

There may be times when you want to copy a file from your hard disk to a floppy disk or copy a file from one directory to another. The File Manager makes it easy to copy files, especially if you are using a mouse. With the mouse, you can drag the file icon for the file you want to copy, to the location to which you want to copy the file. For example, if you want to copy the C:\WINDOWS\README.WRI file to a disk in your drive A, simply drag the file from the WINDOWS directory to the drive A icon.

To copy a file using the mouse, hold down the Ctrl key and drag the file to the destination (onc of the drives or a directory).

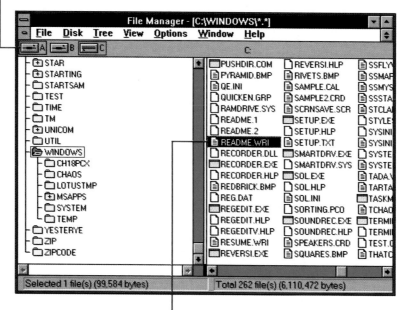

Select the file that you want to copy.

Copying Files

1 In the list of files and directories, select the file you want to copy.

2 Click the File menu, or press **Alt+F**.

3 Click Copy, or press **C**.

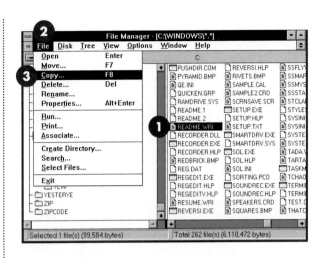

4 In the Copy dialog box, type the destination directory or drive.

5 Click on the **OK** button, or press **Enter**.

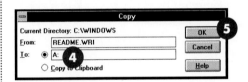
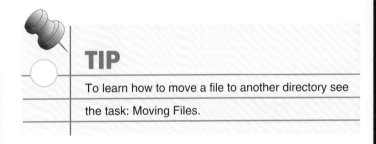

QUICK REFRESHER

Drag: Point to an item, and then press and hold the mouse button as you move the mouse, thereby dragging the item around the display. When finished dragging, release the mouse button.

TIP

To learn how to move a file to another directory see the task: Moving Files.

File Manager

77

COPYING FILES

Exercise

To practice copying files, put a disk in drive A (or B) and copy the file README.WRI to the disk. README.WRI can be found in the C:/WINDOWS directory.

1 Select the **C:/WINDOWS** directory by clicking it on or pressing the down arrow key until you highlight it.

2 In the list of files and directories, select **README.WRI** by clicking or pressing **Tab** and then the arrows until you highlight it.

3 Select the **File** menu by clicking it or pressing **C**.

4 Choose Copy.

5 In the Copy dialog box, type **A:** or **B:** as the destination disk.

6 Click on the **OK** button, or press **Enter**.

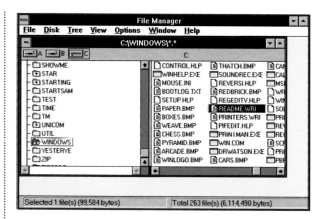

TIP

To copy a file, press and hold down **Ctrl**, and drag the file or directory icon to a directory icon, drive icon, or minimized directory window. If you are copying a file to a different drive, you can drag the file icon without pressing CTRL.

OPENING ANOTHER DIRECTORY WINDOW

Why Open Another Directory Window?

When copying or moving files, it is useful to have more than one directory window open. For example, you might want to copy files by dragging a file or group of files from one directory to another but because of screen size limitations you cannot see all the directories and files in one window. Therefore, you could open a new directory window that you can use to display the files you want to copy, while your original window can be used to display the directory you want to copy the files to. You can open another directory window by selecting a drive icon or by choosing New Window from the Window menu. The new window has the same display settings as the one that was active before you opened the new window.

If you want to open a directory window that displays only the contents of a particular directory, press and hold down **Shift** while you double-click the directory icon in the Directory Tree. A new directory window appears, displaying the contents of that directory.

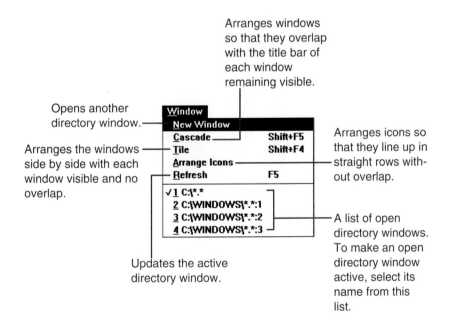

Arranges windows so that they overlap with the title bar of each window remaining visible.

Opens another directory window.

Arranges the windows side by side with each window visible and no overlap.

Arranges icons so that they line up in straight rows without overlap.

Updates the active directory window.

A list of open directory windows. To make an open directory window active, select its name from this list.

OPENING ANOTHER DIRECTORY WINDOW

Opening another Directory Window

1 Click on the Window menu, or press **Alt+W**.

2 Click on New Window, or press **N**.

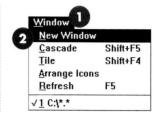

Exercise

To practice opening directory windows, select the **C:\WINDOWS** directory and open another directory window.

1 Select **C:\WINDOWS** from the left side of the directory window by clicking on its icon or pressing the up or down arrow keys to highlight it.

2 Click on the Window menu, or press **Alt+W**.

3 Click on New Window, or press **N**.

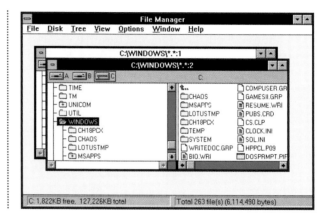

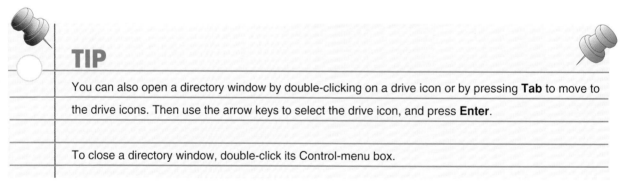

TIP

You can also open a directory window by double-clicking on a drive icon or by pressing **Tab** to move to the drive icons. Then use the arrow keys to select the drive icon, and press **Enter**.

To close a directory window, double-click its Control-menu box.

MOVING FILES

Why *Move* Files?

As you organize your files and directories, you may want to move some files from one directory to another or from one disk to another. Moving is different from copying a file. When you copy a file, you leave the original file intact in its original location. When you move a file, you take it from the source location and actually place it in a new location.

The easiest way to move a file or group of files is with a mouse. You can move files quickly by selecting the file while holding down the **Shift** key and then dragging it to the destination. You can also use the **File Move** command to move a file.

To display the Move dialog box, select File and choose Move. Or press F7.

Select the file you want to move before displaying the Move dialog box.

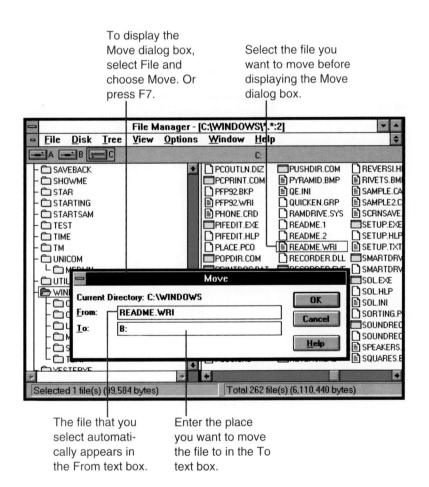

The file that you select automatically appears in the From text box.

Enter the place you want to move the file to in the To text box.

MOVING FILES

Moving Files

1 Select the file or files you want to move.

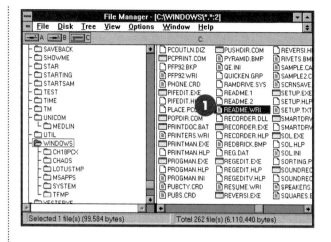

2 Click on the File menu, or press **Alt+F**.

3 Click Move, or press **M**.

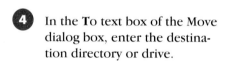

4 In the To text box of the Move dialog box, enter the destination directory or drive.

5 Choose **OK**, or press **ENTER**.

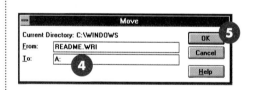

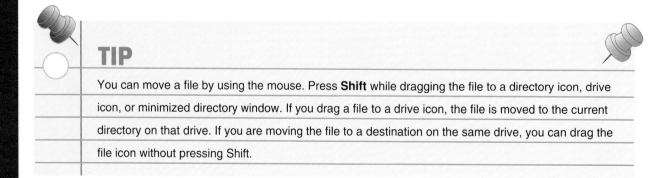

TIP

You can move a file by using the mouse. Press **Shift** while dragging the file to a directory icon, drive icon, or minimized directory window. If you drag a file to a drive icon, the file is moved to the current directory on that drive. If you are moving the file to a destination on the same drive, you can drag the file icon without pressing Shift.

Exercise

To practice moving files put a disk in drive A (or B) and move the file README.WRI to the disk. README.WRI can be found in the C:\WINDOWS directory.

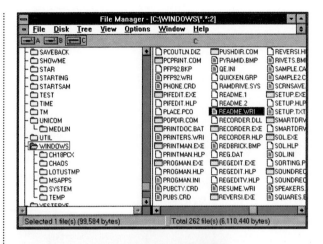

1 Select the **C:\WINDOWS** directory by clicking the icon or pressing the up or down arrow keys to highlight it.

2 In the list of files and directories, click on **README.WRI**, or press **Tab** and the arrow keys to highlight it.

3 Click on the File menu or press **Alt+F**.

4 Click on Move, or press **M**.

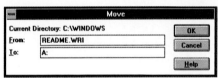

5 In the Move dialog box, type **A:** or **B:** as the destination disk.

6 Click the **OK** button, or press **Enter**.

QUICK REFRESHER

To select a directory and then select a file, click on a directory icon in the Directory Tree (the left side of the directory window). If you are using the keyboard, press **Tab** to move to the Directory Tree, and then use the up or down arrow keys to select a directory. Click on the file of your choice in the right side of the directory window, or if you are using the keyboard, press **Tab** to move to the right side, and then use the arrow keys to highlight (select) a file.

File Manager

SEARCHING FOR A FILE

Why Search for a File?

To open, copy, move, or delete files from your disks you may need to search for the files. File Manager allows you to search for files or groups of files that you have saved on your diskettes or hard drive by using the **File Search** command. If files are found, they are listed in the Search Results window. You can select files in this window to perform such tasks as copying, deleting, moving, and printing files.

The Search dialog box is displayed by selecting File Search.

In the Search for box, you can enter the name of the file or use the wild card character * to search for files with the same extension.

The Start From Text box automatically contains the name of the current directory.

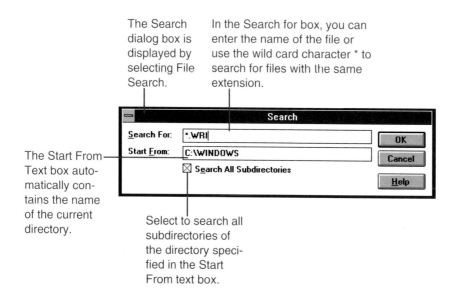

Select to search all subdirectories of the directory specified in the Start From text box.

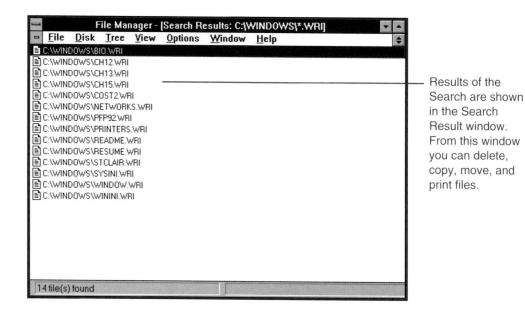

Results of the Search are shown in the Search Result window. From this window you can delete, copy, move, and print files.

Searching for a File

1 Click on the directory from which you want to start the search or press the up or down arrow keys to highlight the directory.

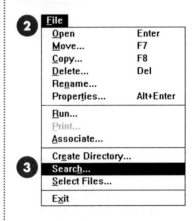

2 Click on the File menu, or press **Alt+F**.

3 Click on Search, or press **H**.

4 In the Search For text box of the Search dialog box, specify what you want to search for.

5 Click the **OK** button, or press **Enter**.

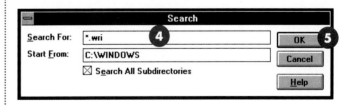

85

SEARCHING FOR A FILE

Exercise

Practice using the search command by searching for all files in the C:\WINDOWS directory that have the WRI extension.

1 Select the **C:\WINDOWS** directory by clicking its icon or by pressing the up or down arrow keys to highlight it.

2 Click on **File** menu or press **Alt+F**.

3 Click on Searc**h** or press **H**.

4 In the **S**earch For text box of the Search dialog box, type ***.WRI**.

5 Select the **OK** button, or press **Enter**.

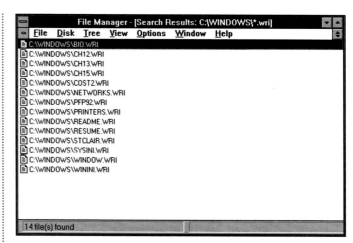

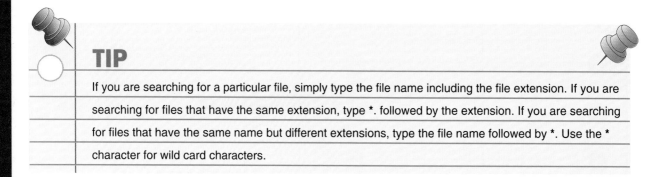

TIP

If you are searching for a particular file, simply type the file name including the file extension. If you are searching for files that have the same extension, type *. followed by the extension. If you are searching for files that have the same name but different extensions, type the file name followed by *. Use the * character for wild card characters.

Why Format a Disk?

Before you can use most disks, you must first format them. Formatting prepares the disk for use with your computer. When you format a disk, you are preparing the disk so that data can be stored on it. Formatting creates a storage layout and deletes any previous information stored on it. Unless you purchase a preformatted disk, you cannot use a disk without first formatting it.

You can enter a Volume label for the disk. A volume label is a name for the disk. It can be up to 11 characters.

Select the drive you want to format.

Select the disk capacity.

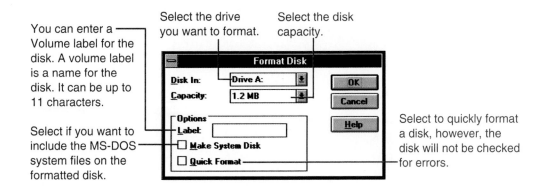

Select if you want to include the MS-DOS system files on the formatted disk.

Select to quickly format a disk, however, the disk will not be checked for errors.

Formatting a Disk

1 Insert the disk that you want to format into a drive.

2 Click on the **Disk** menu, or press **Alt+D**.

3 Click on Format Disk, or press **F**.

File Manager

FORMATTING A DISK

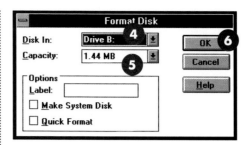

4 If the drive containing the disk is different from that shown in **Disk In** box, select the appropriate drive letter by clicking on the **D**isk In down arrow to display the drop-down list of drive letters and then clicking on a drive letter. If you are using the keyboard, press the **Tab** key to select the **D**isk In box, and then use the down arrow to select the drive letter.

5 If the capacity of the disk is different from that shown in the **C**apacity box, select the appropriate capacity by clicking on the **C**apacity down arrow to display the drop-down list of disk capacities and then clicking on a capacity. If you are using the keyboard, press the **Tab** key until you select the Capacity box, and then use the down arrow to select the capacity.

6 Click on the **OK** button, or press **Enter**.

PART 4

Print Manager

Print Manager is an application that helps you to print your letters, worksheets, and graphs. In fact, all of your printing needs are managed by the Print Manager. When you print from a Windows application, the application sends information to the Print Manager that describes the file that you want to print, the printer you want to use, and the fonts included in the document. Then the Print Manager controls the printing of your document and frees up the computer so that you can continue working with Windows applications while you are printing.

This part of the book shows you how to perform four basic Print Manager tasks. After working through this section, you will be able to use the Print Manager to see what documents Print Manager has yet to print, to delete a previous print job that you sent to the printer, to change printing options and settings, and to switch from one printer to another.

- Viewing the Print Queue
- Deleting a Print Job
- Changing the Printer Setup
- Choosing a Different Printer

VIEWING THE PRINT QUEUE

Why View the Print Queue?

One of the advantages of the Print Manager is that you can print documents in succession. By working with your Windows applications, you can print a spreadsheet, then a letter, then a graph, and each job will be sent to the Print Manager, forming sort of a line or queue. That's what a *print queue* is: a list of documents that have been sent to the Print Manager, each waiting its turn to be printed.

The print queue is displayed in the Print Manager window as a list of information about documents waiting to be printed. The information includes the time and date you sent the document to the printer and its file size. After you begin printing a document, the Print Manager icon appears at the bottom of your Windows screen. You view the print queue by restoring the Print Manager icon to a window. To view the Print Manager when you are not printing, select its icon from the Main Group window.

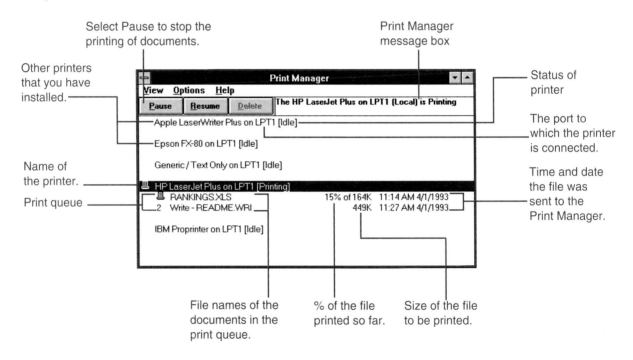

Select Pause to stop the printing of documents.

Print Manager message box

Other printers that you have installed.

Status of printer

The port to which the printer is connected.

Name of the printer.

Print queue

Time and date the file was sent to the Print Manager.

File names of the documents in the print queue.

% of the file printed so far.

Size of the file to be printed.

LEARNING THE LINGO

Print queue: A list of documents that have been sent to the Print Manager.

Port: A connection on the computer to which your printer is attached.

Viewing the Print Queue

Print Manager

1 Double-click on the **Print Manager** icon, or press **Alt+Tab** until you select the **Print Manager** (a box will be displayed in the screen containing the Print Manager icon—when you release **Alt+Tab**—the Print Manager window will be displayed).

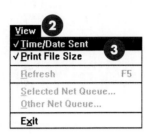

2 To display the time and date or file size in the print queue, click on the View menu, or press **Alt+V**.

3 Click on Time/Date Sent or **P**rint File Size, or press **T** or **P**. A check mark next to these commands means that the command is in effect.

Print Manager

DELETING A PRINT JOB

Why Delete a Print Job?

After sending a document to the Print Manager, you may decide to delete that file from the print queue. For example, after using the **File Print** command of a particular application, you may discover that you specified the wrong pages or possibly the wrong document to be printed. You can quickly correct your mistake by deleting that particular print job and stopping the document from being printed out from the Print Manager.

Select Delete to cancel a particular print job.

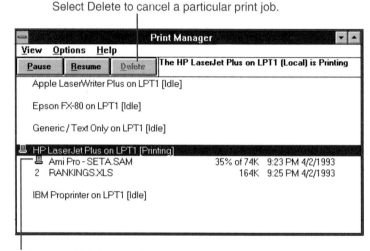

Select the print job to be deleted.

Deleting a Print Job

1 Restore the **Print Manager** icon by double-clicking on it or by pressing **Alt+Tab** until you select the **Print Manager**.

Print Manager

2 In the Print Manager window, select the print job you want to delete by clicking on it or using the down arrow key to highlight it.

3 Click the Delete button, or press **Alt+D**.

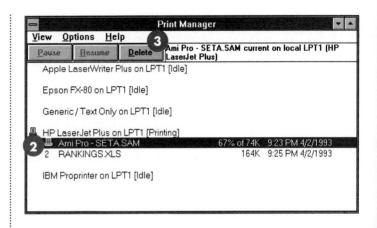

4 Click on the **OK** button, or press **Enter** to confirm the deletion.

TIP

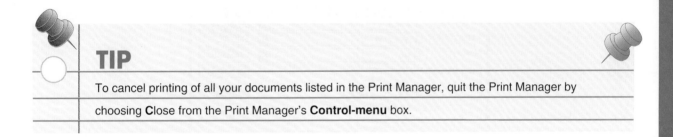

To cancel printing of all your documents listed in the Print Manager, quit the Print Manager by choosing **C**lose from the Print Manager's **Control-menu** box.

Print Manager

CHANGING THE PRINTER SETUP

Why Change the Printer Setup?

Many printers have various settings, such as page orientation, paper size, and graphics resolution that you can specify using Print Manager. These settings allow you to get the printing results you want. To change printer settings, you can choose **P**rinter Setup from the **O**ptions menu of the Print Manager. The **P**rinter Setup command allows you to change printers and to display the Printer Setup dialog box for your installed printer so that you can change print settings.

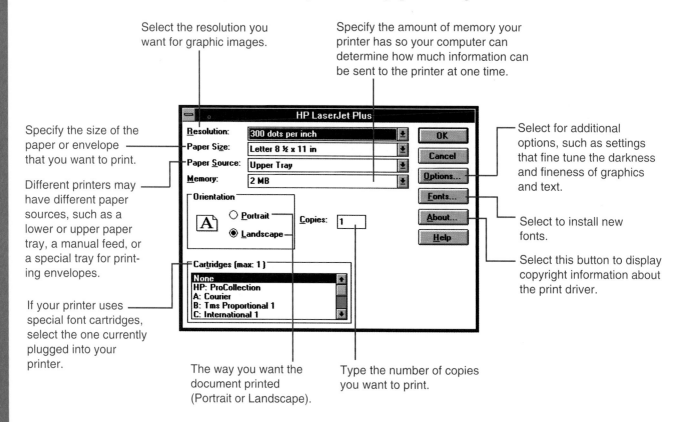

Select the resolution you want for graphic images.

Specify the amount of memory your printer has so your computer can determine how much information can be sent to the printer at one time.

Specify the size of the paper or envelope that you want to print.

Different printers may have different paper sources, such as a lower or upper paper tray, a manual feed, or a special tray for printing envelopes.

If your printer uses special font cartridges, select the one currently plugged into your printer.

Select for additional options, such as settings that fine tune the darkness and fineness of graphics and text.

Select to install new fonts.

Select this button to display copyright information about the print driver.

The way you want the document printed (Portrait or Landscape).

Type the number of copies you want to print.

HP LaserJet Plus

Resolution: 300 dots per inch
Paper Size: Letter 8 ½ x 11 in
Paper Source: Upper Tray
Memory: 2 MB

Orientation
○ Portrait
● Landscape

Copies: 1

Cartridges (max: 1)
None
HP: ProCollection
A: Courier
B: Tms Proportional 1
C: International 1

OK
Cancel
Options...
Fonts...
About...
Help

Changing the Printer Setup

1 Open the **Main** group window, and double-click on the **Print Manager** icon, or use the arrow keys to select the icon and press **Enter**.

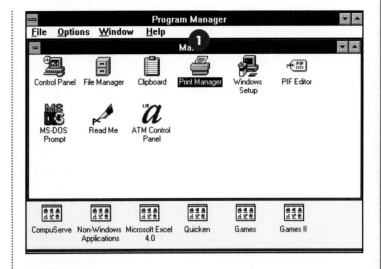

2 Click on the **O**ptions menu, or press **Alt+O**.

3 Click on **P**rinter Setup or press **P**.

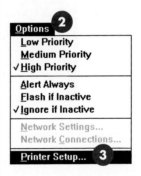

4 From the Installed **P**rinters list box, click on the printer you want to set up, or use the up or down arrow keys to highlight the printer.

5 Click on the **S**etup button or press **Alt+S**.

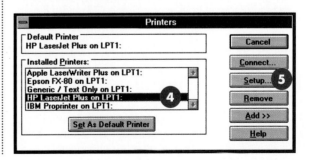

Print Manager

CHANGING THE PRINTER SETUP

6 Select the settings you want to change. If the setting is in a drop-down box (such as **Resolution**), click the down arrow of the setting's box, and click on the setting you want. Or press **Alt+** the selection letter of the setting (for example, the selection letter for **Resolution** is **R**—the underline letter).

7 Click on the **OK** button, or press **Enter**.

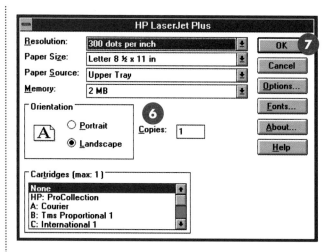

8 Click on the Close button in the Printers dialog box, or press **Esc**.

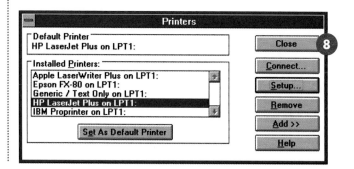

LEARNING THE LINGO

Graphics resolution: The degree of sharpness of a printed graphic image. Resolution is measured in the number of dots per inch (dpi). The more dots per inch, the higher the resolution. Many laser printers can print at 300 dpi.

Paper orientation: The way that you want your document printed across the page. *Portrait* orientation means that your document will be printed across the narrow width of the page (the page is longer than it is wide), while *landscape* orientation means that your document will be printed across the wider part of the page (sideways).

Print driver: A program that controls how your computer interacts with the printer. Print drivers make it possible for your computer to communicate with your printer so that you can use features such as fonts and formatting when printing your documents.

CHOOSING A DIFFERENT PRINTER

Why Choose a Different Printer?

When you install Windows, you can specify the printers on which you plan to work. For example, you might plan printing rough drafts of documents on a dot-matrix printer and only print final documents on your laser printer. For each printer that you want to install, Windows copies a printer driver file to the hard disk of your computer. A printer driver file provides instructions that your computer follows to communicate with your printer.

If you want to change to a different printer, you can use the Print Manager to switch to that other printer. When you switch to another printer, it becomes the *default* printer—the printer that the Print Manager will automatically print to each time you print a document.

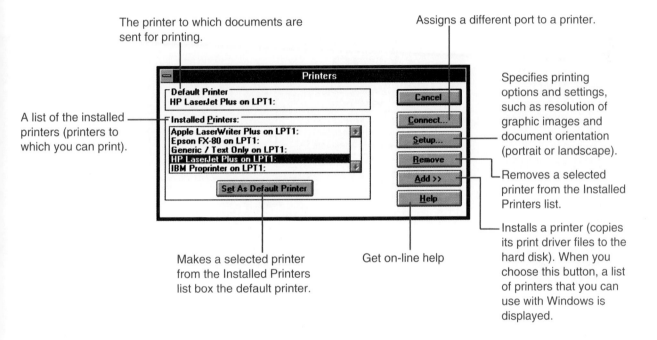

The printer to which documents are sent for printing.

Assigns a different port to a printer.

A list of the installed printers (printers to which you can print).

Specifies printing options and settings, such as resolution of graphic images and document orientation (portrait or landscape).

Removes a selected printer from the Installed Printers list.

Installs a printer (copies its print driver files to the hard disk). When you choose this button, a list of printers that you can use with Windows is displayed.

Makes a selected printer from the Installed Printers list box the default printer.

Get on-line help

Print Manager

Choosing a Different Printer

1 Open the **Main** group window, and double-click on the **Print Manager** icon, or use the arrow keys to select the icon, and press **Enter**.

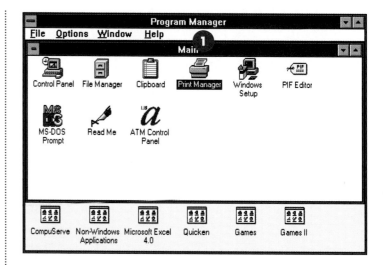

2 Click on the **O**ptions menu, or press **Alt+O**.

3 Click on **P**rinter Setup or press **P**.

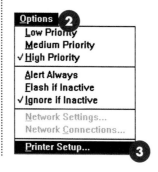

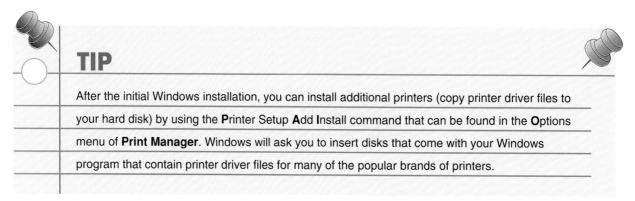

TIP

After the initial Windows installation, you can install additional printers (copy printer driver files to your hard disk) by using the **P**rinter Setup **A**dd **I**nstall command that can be found in the **O**ptions menu of **Print Manager**. Windows will ask you to insert disks that come with your Windows program that contain printer driver files for many of the popular brands of printers.

4 From the Installed **P**rinters list box, click on the printer to which you want to change, or use the up or down arrow keys to highlight the printer.

5 Click on the S**e**t As Default Printer button, or press **E**.

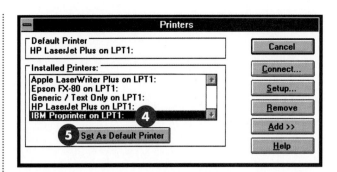

6 Choose the Close button.

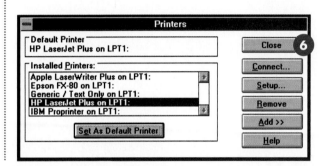

LEARNING THE LINGO

Default printer: The printer that the Print Manager will automatically print to each time you print a document. Despite the fact that you can have more than one printer installed, you can have only one default printer at one time.

Installed Printer: A printer from which you can print. A printer can be installed after its printer driver files have been copied to the hard disk and the command Printer Setup Add from the Print Manager's Option menu has been executed. You can see if a printer is installed by viewing the Installed Printers list in the Printers dialog box.

Port: A connection on the computer to which your printer is attached.

Print driver file: A program that controls how your computer interacts with the printer. Print drivers make it possible for your computer to communicate with your printer so that you can use features such as fonts and formatting when printing your documents.

Print Manager

PART 5

Windows Accessories

This section describes how you can utilize some of the applications found in the Accessories group. If you read through this entire section and work its exercises, you will have a basic understanding of how to work with many of the commonly used applications of the Accessories group. The Accessories applications that are examined in this section include:

Write   A basic word processing program.

Paintbrush   A drawing program that allows you to create, color, edit, and print graphics.

- Opening a Document
- Printing a Document
- Saving a Document
- Entering Text in Write
- Moving the Insertion Point
- Editing Text with Find and Replace
- Selecting Text

- Cutting Text
- Copying and Moving Text
- Formatting Characters
- Drawing a Paintbrush Graphic
- Adding Text to a Paintbrush Graphic
- Saving a Paintbrush Graphic

OPENING A DOCUMENT

Why Open a Document?

In Windows, a *document* is what you create with your applications. For example, a document could be a letter, report, card file, spreadsheet, or drawing. Once you create a document, you save it to recall or open later for revisions or to print. Opening a document recalls a previously saved document. Regardless of which Windows application you are working with, you open a document by using the **File Open** command. The Open dialog box appears from which you can choose the drive and directory containing the document and the file name of the document.

Enter the name of the document you want to open or select the document name from the File Name list box.

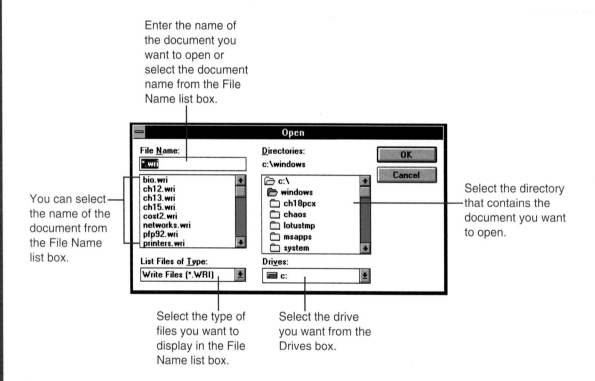

You can select the name of the document from the File Name list box.

Select the directory that contains the document you want to open.

Select the type of files you want to display in the File Name list box.

Select the drive you want from the Drives box.

LEARNING THE LINGO

Document: What you create with your applications such as letters, reports, spreadsheets, or drawings.

Opening a Document

1 Click on the **F**ile menu, or press **Alt+F**.

2 Click on **O**pen, or press **O**.

3 If the document you want to open is on a drive different from the drive shown in the Drives box, select the drive you want by either clicking on the down arrow of the Drives box and clicking on the drive you want or by pressing **Alt+V** to select the Drives box and using the down arrow key to select the drive.

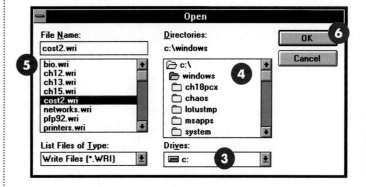

4 If the directory you want is different from the current directory, double-click on the name of the directory you want in the **Directories** list box. Or press **Alt+D** and the up or down arrow keys to select the directory, and then press **Enter**.

5 In the File **N**ame text box, type the name of the document. Or select the file name by clicking on it in the File **N**ame list box or pressing **Tab** until you select the File **N**ame list box, and then use the up and down arrow keys to select the document's file name.

6 Choose the **OK** button, or press **Enter**.

Windows Accessories

PRINTING A DOCUMENT

Why Print a Document?

When you get your document looking the way you want it, you can print a hard copy by using the application's **File Print** command.

The way you print Windows documents is the same for all Window's applications. Windows applications usually allow you to use special setup options, such as what printer to use, the number of pages to print, the orientation of the printout (portrait or landscape), and paper size.

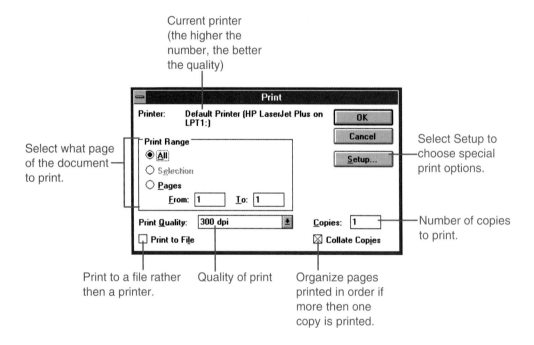

Current printer (the higher the number, the better the quality)

Select what page of the document to print.

Select Setup to choose special print options.

Number of copies to print.

Print to a file rather then a printer.

Quality of print

Organize pages printed in order if more then one copy is printed.

Printing a Document

1 Click on the File menu, or press **Alt+F**.

2 Click on **Print**, or press **P**.

3 If the application allows you to choose special print options, a Print dialog box will be displayed. You will have the choice of selecting several printing options.

4 Once you have finished selecting options, click on **OK**, or press **Enter** to begin printing.

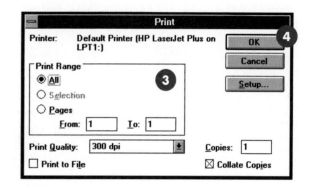

SAVING A DOCUMENT

Why Save a Document?

As you create a document, it resides in your computer's internal memory, which is a *temporary* storage space. If you want to save your work in a permanent way, you must save on a floppy disk or on your hard disk. Your documents can be saved under a file name so that you can later open them to revise or print them. File names may be up to eight characters and may not contain spaces or punctuation. An extension, consisting of a period (.) and one to three characters, can be added to a file name. For example, if you create a document to be named MEMO, you can add the letters TXT to signify that the file contains text (MEMO.TXT). Some applications will add a common extension to a file name if you choose not to add one when you name the file. For example, Write will add the extension .WRI to the end of a file name.

To save a document for the first time, use **File Save**. If you want to save the current document (which has been previously saved and named) under a new name, you must use the **File Save As** command.

Select a directory
into which you want
to save the file.

Type a file name
in the File Name
text box.

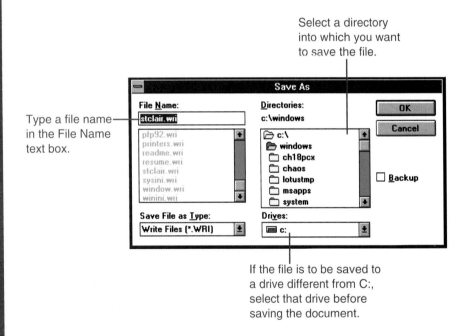

If the file is to be saved to
a drive different from C:,
select that drive before
saving the document.

LEARNING THE LINGO

Extension: A period (.) and up to three characters that can be added to the end of a file name. For example, the file MEMO could be named MEMO.TXT to show that the file contains text (TXT).

Saving a Document

1. Click on **File**, or press **Alt+F**.

2. Click on Save **As**, or press **A**.

3. Type a file name in the File **N**ame text box.

4. In the **Directories** list box, click on the directory to which you want to save the file. Or press Alt+D to select the **Directories** list box, and use the down arrow key to select a directory.

5. If you want to save on another drive, click on the **Drives** drop-down list box, and click on a drive. If you are using the keyboard, press **Alt+V**, and use the up and down arrow keys to select a drive.

6. Click on the **OK** button, or press **Enter**.

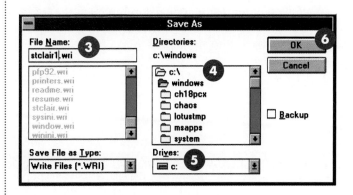

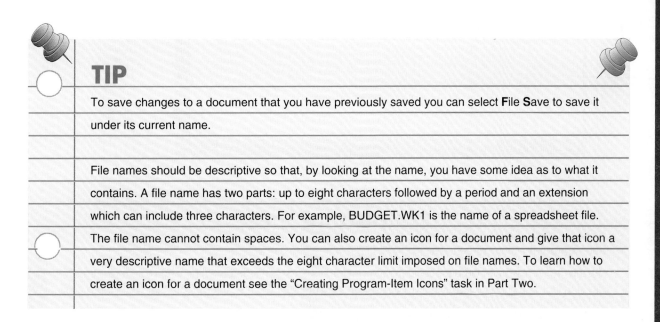

TIP

To save changes to a document that you have previously saved you can select **File** **S**ave to save it under its current name.

File names should be descriptive so that, by looking at the name, you have some idea as to what it contains. A file name has two parts: up to eight characters followed by a period and an extension which can include three characters. For example, BUDGET.WK1 is the name of a spreadsheet file. The file name cannot contain spaces. You can also create an icon for a document and give that icon a very descriptive name that exceeds the eight character limit imposed on file names. To learn how to create an icon for a document see the "Creating Program-Item Icons" task in Part Two.

Windows Accessories

ENTERING TEXT IN WRITE

How to Enter Text in Write?

Windows comes with a word processing application in the Accessories group called Write, where you can create memos, letters, resumes, reports, and so on. When you start Write, you will see a blank document ready for you to enter text, just like if you were using a typewriter. The main difference is you don't have to press Enter at the end of each line, because Write automatically starts a new line when text reaches the right margin (this is called *wrapping*). You need to press Enter only when you want to start a new paragraph.

When you enter text it appears on screen at the location of the *insertion point*. The insertion point is marked by a blinking vertical line. The end of the document is marked by a short horizontal line.

The insertion point is the place where text will be inserted when you type. It is a flashing vertical bar.

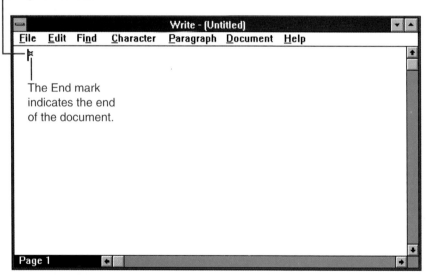

The End mark indicates the end of the document.

108

Entering Text in Write

To run Write follow these steps:

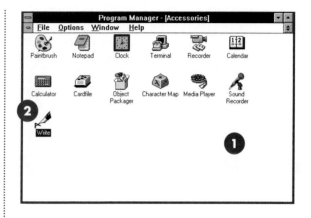

1 Position the mouse pointer over the Accessories group window icon and double-click it (or if the group window is open, click anywhere on the window to make it the active window). If you are using the keyboard, press **Ctrl+Tab** until you select the group window, and then press **Enter**. If the Accessories group window is not open, select **W**indow and then select Accessories from the group list.

2 Double-click on the **Write** icon. Or press the arrow keys until you select the **Write** icon, and then press **Enter**. The Write application's window opens and the program is up and running.

3 At the insertion point, start typing your document.

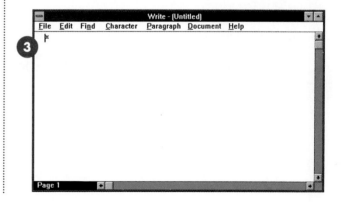

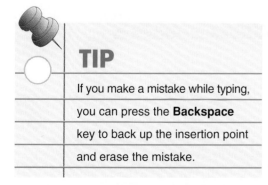

TIP

If you make a mistake while typing, you can press the **Backspace** key to back up the insertion point and erase the mistake.

Windows Accessories

MOVING THE INSERTION POINT

Why Move the Insertion Point?

To move quickly around the document (to insert, delete, and edit text), you can use the mouse to move the insertion point. Simply point to a location with your mouse, and click. With the keyboard, you can move the insertion point by using the up, down, right and left arrow keys. You can also use the Spacebar to move the insertion point one space at a time.

If you press **Enter**, the insertion point moves to the beginning of the next line and begins a new paragraph. You can also use the following special keys and keyboard combinations to move the insertion point around your document.

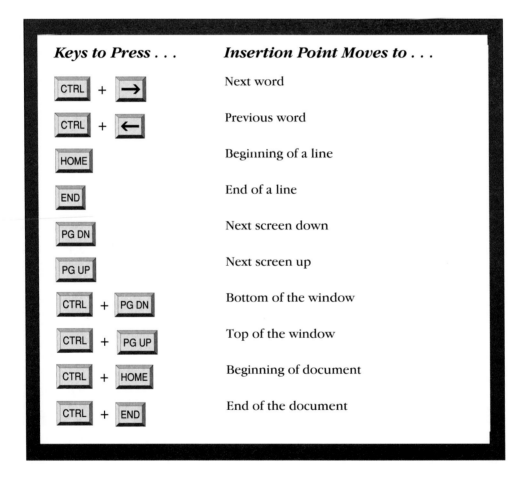

Keys to Press . . .	Insertion Point Moves to . . .
CTRL + →	Next word
CTRL + ←	Previous word
HOME	Beginning of a line
END	End of a line
PG DN	Next screen down
PG UP	Next screen up
CTRL + PG DN	Bottom of the window
CTRL + PG UP	Top of the window
CTRL + HOME	Beginning of document
CTRL + END	End of the document

TIP

For a shortcut way to move to specific pages, press **F4** to display the Go To dialog box.

If you want to move the insertion point to a specific page, you can use the Find Go To Page command, and then specify the page number.

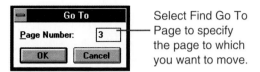

Select Find Go To Page to specify the page to which you want to move.

Moving the Insertion Point to a Specific Page

1 Click on the Find menu, or press **Alt+N**.

2 Click on Go to Page, or press **G**.

3 In the **Page Number** box, enter the number of the page to which you want to go to.

4 Click on **OK**, or press **Enter**.

Exercise

Open the Write file named **README.WRI**, which can be found in the **Windows** directory. Move the insertion point to the beginning of page 4. (To make this exercise work, you may have to repaginate the pages of README.WRI prior to using the Find Go To Page command. To repaginate the document, select File Repaginate. The Repaginate command divides your document into pages.)

1 Open **README.WRI** by selecting File Open and choosing the file from the File Name List.

2 Repaginate the document by selecting File Repaginate.

3 Select Find Go to Page to move to page 4 by clicking on the Find menu and clicking Go to Page or by pressing **F4**.

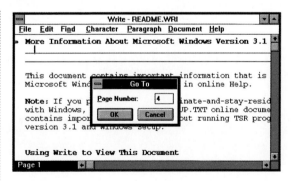

EDITING TEXT WITH FIND AND REPLACE

Why Use Find and Replace?

Since we all make mistakes, there are times when we need to edit the text we have typed in our documents. You can edit your document by moving the insertion point to the location where you need to make a change and then make the corrections.

You can also use the Find Replace command to locate each occurrence of a word or phrase and replace each occurrence. Find Replace is a very quick and efficient way to make global changes to a document. With this command you can search for text up to 255 characters in length and change all occurrences of that text or only certain occurrences of the text.

When you use Find Replace to make changes to your document, Write begins its search from the insertion point. Therefore, before you execute this command , be sure you have properly positioned your insertion point because Write will search forward from the insertion point. Also, if you only want to search a section of your document, you can do that by selecting the text in that section of the document. For details on how to select text, see the next task, "Selecting Text".

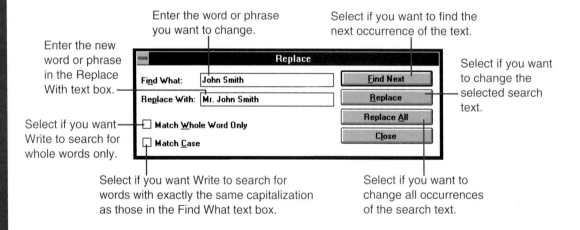

Enter the word or phrase you want to change.

Select if you want to find the next occurrence of the text.

Enter the new word or phrase in the Replace With text box.

Select if you want to change the selected search text.

Select if you want Write to search for whole words only.

Select if you want Write to search for words with exactly the same capitalization as those in the Find What text box.

Select if you want to change all occurrences of the search text.

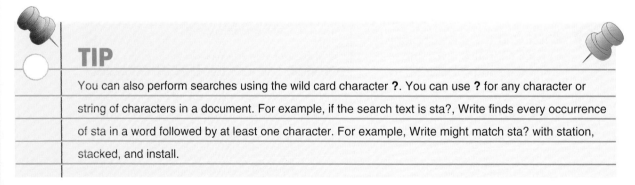

TIP

You can also perform searches using the wild card character **?**. You can use **?** for any character or string of characters in a document. For example, if the search text is sta?, Write finds every occurrence of sta in a word followed by at least one character. For example, Write might match sta? with station, stacked, and install.

Finding and Replacing Text

1 Click on the Find menu, or press **Alt+N**.

2 Click on Replace or press E.

3 In the Find What text box, type the text to search for in the document.

4 In the Replace With text box, type the new text.

5 To find entire words only, select the Match Whole Word Only check box by clicking on it, or press **Alt+W**.

6 To match capitalization exactly, select the Match Case check box by clicking on it, or press **Alt+C**.

7 Choose one of the following command buttons by clicking on it or by pressing **Alt +** the underlined letter on the buttons.

8 To close the Replace dialog box, choose the Close button by clicking on the button, or press **Alt+L** or presss **Esc**.

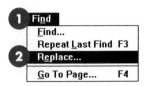

LEARNING THE LINGO

Find Next: If you want to find the next occurrence of the search text.

Replace: If you want to change the selected search text.

Replace All: If you want to change all the occurrences of the search text in the document.

Replace Selection: If you want to change all the occurrences of the search text in the selected portion of the document (if you selected a section of the document in which you want to search).

Windows Accessories

SELECTING TEXT

Why Select Text?

To edit or format text in a Write document, you need to first *select* it. To select a word or a few words you can position the insertion point at the beginning of the word or at the beginning of the first word in the phrase that you want to select. The easiest way to select text is with the mouse. You can select the text by holding down the mouse button and moving the pointer over the text. You will see the screen darken where you have selected the text. You can also select text with the keyboard by positioning the insertion point and then highlighting the text by holding down the SHIFT key while you use the arrow keys to move over the text.

You can select blocks of text by clicking on the selection area. The selection area is an invisible section of the Write window that extends vertically along the left margin. The mouse pointer changes to an arrow shape and slants to the right when inside the selection area. Below is a summary of types of text selections you can make using the selection area.

Selections Text	Procedure
A single line	In the selection area, point to a line and click the mouse button.
Several lines	In the selection area, point to a line and drag the pointer up or down within the selection area.
A paragraph	In the selection area, point to a paragraph and double-click.
Several paragraphs	In the selection area, point to a paragraph and double-click and hold down the mouse button. Drag the pointer up or down the selection area.
A range of text	Select the starting line or paragraph. Press and hold down **Shift** while clicking on the last line or paragraph from the selection area. Write selects everything between the two points.
The entire document	Press and hold down **Ctrl**, and, with the pointer in the selection area, click.

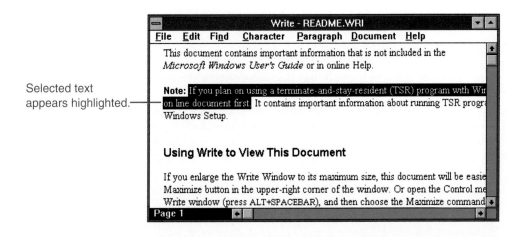

Selected text appears highlighted.

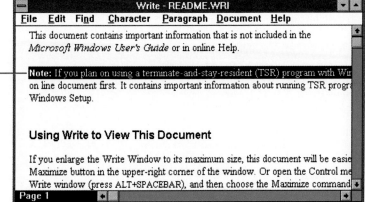

Selection area is the far left edge of the Write window. When you move the mouse pointer to the selection area, its shape changes to a small arrow starting to the right.

Selecting Text

1 Position the insertion point where you would like to begin selecting text.

2 Hold down the mouse button and move the pointer over the text you want to select. When you reach the end of the selection, release the mouse button. If you are using the keyboard, highlight the text by holding down the **Shift** key while using the arrow keys to move over the text you want to select.

LEARNING THE LINGO

Select: To mark a word, sentence, paragraph, or other item in a document.

Selection area: An invisible section of the Write window that extends vertically along the left margin. You can click on this area to select text.

115

CUTTING TEXT

Why Cut Text?

As you prepare, revise, and edit documents you may need to delete some text. When you delete text, Windows places the deleted text in the Clipboard (a temporary storage area for deleted and copied data). To learn how to view the contents of the Clipboard, see the "Viewing Clipboard Contents" task. You can delete text by selecting the text or graphics and then choosing Edit Cut. The Cut command places the cut selection onto the Clipboard, replacing the previous Clipboard contents. The Edit Cut command is available only when text or graphics are selected. If you have not selected text or graphics, the Cut choice will appear dimmed on the Edit menu and will be disabled.

Select Edit Cut, or
press the Ctrl+X
shortcut to delete text.

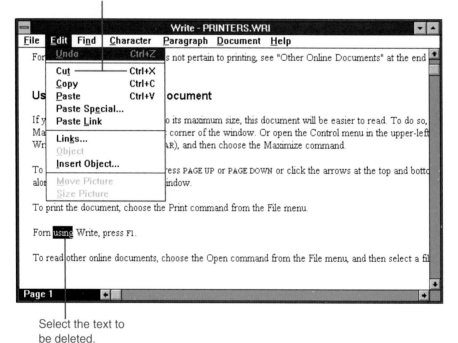

Select the text to
be deleted.

TIP

If you want to delete selected text permanently, use the **Del** key by pressing **Del**, the text will not be placed on the Clipboard.

Cutting Text

1 Select the text that you want to delete. To learn how to select text see the previous task, "Selecting Text."

2 Click on the **E**dit menu, or press **Alt+E**.

3 Click on Cu**t**, or press **T**.

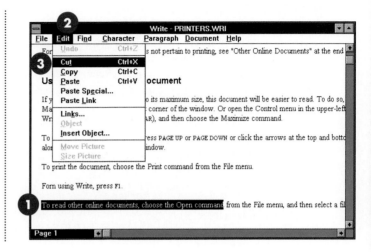

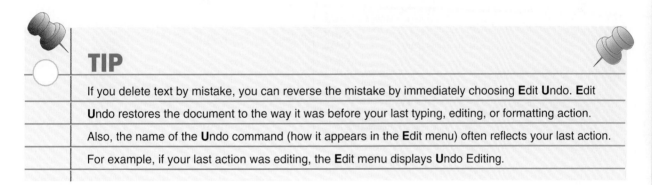

TIP

If you delete text by mistake, you can reverse the mistake by immediately choosing **E**dit **U**ndo. **E**dit **U**ndo restores the document to the way it was before your last typing, editing, or formatting action.

Also, the name of the **U**ndo command (how it appears in the **E**dit menu) often reflects your last action.

For example, if your last action was editing, the **E**dit menu displays **U**ndo Editing.

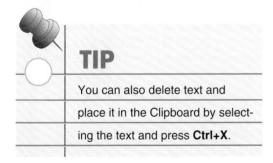

TIP

You can also delete text and place it in the Clipboard by selecting the text and press **Ctrl+X**.

Windows Accessories

COPYING AND MOVING TEXT

Why Copy and Move Text?

After typing your document, you may want to rearrange or reorganize it by copying and moving text around in your document. You copy text by selecting the text and using the **Edit Copy** command. A copy of the text is placed on the Clipboard. Then you can paste a copy of the text to any place on your Write document by using **Edit Paste**.

To move text, you select it, cut it, and then paste it to the location you want it moved. This is done by using the **Edit Cut** and **Edit Paste** commands.

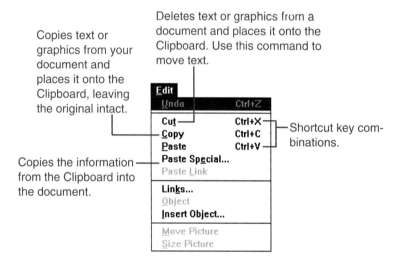

Deletes text or graphics from a document and places it onto the Clipboard. Use this command to move text.

Copies text or graphics from your document and places it onto the Clipboard, leaving the original intact.

Copies the information from the Clipboard into the document.

Shortcut key combinations.

LEARNING THE LINGO

Copy: To select text or objects and use the **E**dit **C**opy command to place a duplicate on the Clipboard so that it can be pasted to another location in the document or into another application by using the **E**dit **P**aste command.

Cutting: To Select text or objects then use the **E**dit Cu**t** command to remove the item from the document and place it on the Windows Clipboard.

Moving: To select text or objects and reposition it in the document by using the **E**dit **C**opy and **E**dit **P**aste command.

Pasting: To transfer contents of the Clipboard (text or objects) into a document by using the Edit Paste command.

Copying and Moving Text

1 Select the text you want to copy.

2 Click on the **E**dit menu, or press **Alt+E**.

3 Click on **C**opy (or press **C**) to copy text; or click on Cu**t** (or press **T**) to move text.

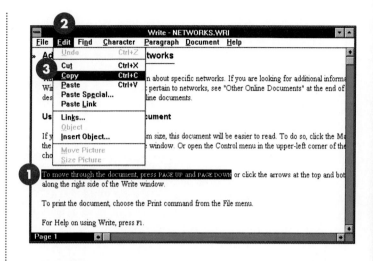

4 Move the insertion point to the place you want the copied or moved text to appear. For information on how to move the insertion point see the "Moving the Insertion Point" task.

5 Click on the **E**dit menu, or press **Alt+E**.

6 Click on **P**aste, or press **P**.

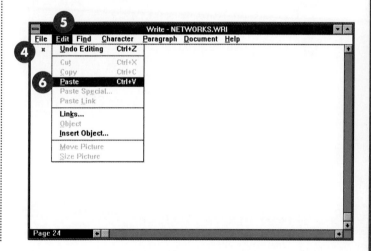

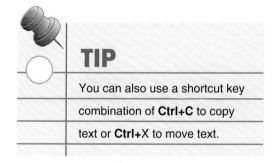

TIP

You can also use a shortcut key combination of **Ctrl+C** to copy text or **Ctrl+X** to move text.

QUICK REFRESHER

Selecting Text

1. Position the insertion point where you want to begin selecting text.

2. Hold down the mouse button and move the pointer over the text you want to select. When you reach the end of the selection, release to mouse button.

Windows Accessories

COPYING AND MOVING TEXT

Exercise

To practice moving text in a document, run Write, and type the following sentence just as is: **The red red fox jumped over the wagon.** Then edit the sentence by moving the extra red to just before wagon.

1 Type the following sentence just as is: **The red red fox jumped over the wagon.**

2 Select **red**.

3 Click on the **E**dit menu, or press **Alt+E**.

4 Click on Cu**t**, or press **T**.

5 Move the insertion point to just before the word wagon.

6 Click on the **E**dit menu, or press **Alt+E**.

7 Click on **P**aste, or press **P**.

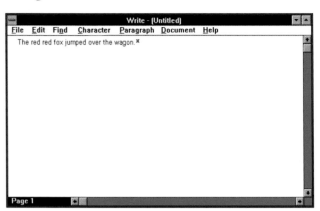

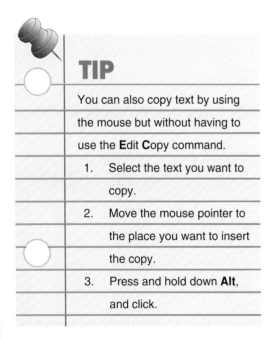

TIP

You can also copy text by using the mouse but without having to use the **E**dit **C**opy command.

1. Select the text you want to copy.

2. Move the mouse pointer to the place you want to insert the copy.

3. Press and hold down **Alt**, and click.

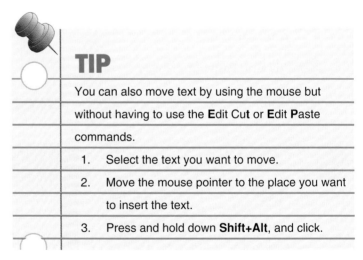

TIP

You can also move text by using the mouse but without having to use the **E**dit Cut or **E**dit **P**aste commands.

1. Select the text you want to move.

2. Move the mouse pointer to the place you want to insert the text.

3. Press and hold down **Shift+Alt**, and click.

FORMATTING CHARACTERS

Why Format Characters?

As you create documents, you will develop a vision as to how you want the finished product to look. You may want to underline some text, use bold typeface and italics, and change fonts. You can get your document looking the way you want by using the commands on the Character menu.

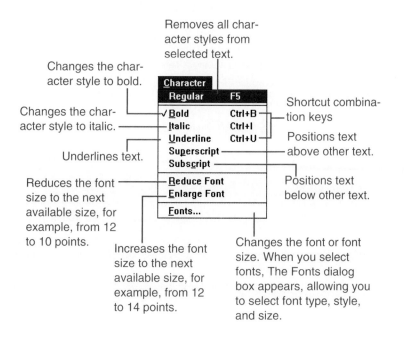

Removes all character styles from selected text.

Changes the character style to bold.

Changes the character style to italic.

Underlines text.

Reduces the font size to the next available size, for example, from 12 to 10 points.

Increases the font size to the next available size, for example, from 12 to 14 points.

Shortcut combination keys

Positions text above other text.

Positions text below other text.

Changes the font or font size. When you select fonts, The Fonts dialog box appears, allowing you to select font type, style, and size.

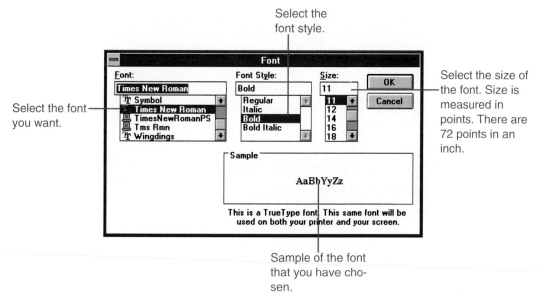

Select the font style.

Select the font you want.

Select the size of the font. Size is measured in points. There are 72 points in an inch.

Sample of the font that you have chosen.

121

FORMATTING CHARACTERS

Formatting Characters

1 Select the text you want to format.

2 Click on the **Character** menu, or press **Alt+C**.

3 Select the format you want. For example, if you want to make your text box, click on **B**old, or press **B**. If you select Fonts, the Font dialog box will appear. To learn how to make selections in a dialog box, see the "Working with Dialog Boxes" task.

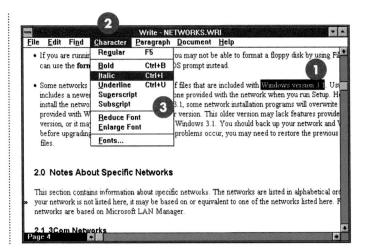

LEARNING THE LINGO

Fonts: Characters of a given size and design. For example, this is a font called Courier that is 12 points in size.

Point size: The height of a printed character. A 72 point font is an inch tall. A 36 point font is a half inch tall.

TIP

To cancel a particular character format:

1. Select the text whose format you want to cancel.

2. From the **C**haracter menu, choose the format (it will have a check mark next to it).

To cancel all character formats that have been applied to text:

1. Select the text whose styles you want to cancel.

2. From the **C**haracter menu, choose Re**g**ular.

A shortcut to cancel all formatting on text is to select the text and then press **F5**.

DRAWING A PAINTBRUSH GRAPHIC

Why Draw a Paintbrush Graphic?

Paintbrush is a drawing application that you can find in the Accessories group. You can use Paintbrush to create graphics that you can add to documents prepared with other applications. For example, you can draw a picture and insert it into a Write document.

Paintbrush is one of the Windows applications that is much easier to use if you utilize the mouse. Much of the drawing and coloring is done by dragging the mouse pointer around the screen. Before you start drawing in the drawing area, you need to first select a tool to draw, like you would need to pick up a pencil or paintbrush before you can being to draw.

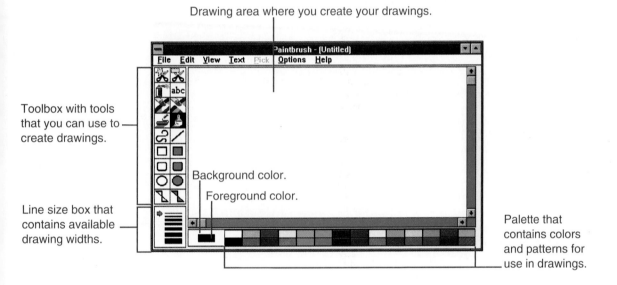

Drawing area where you create your drawings.

Toolbox with tools that you can use to create drawings.

Line size box that contains available drawing widths.

Background color.

Foreground color.

Palette that contains colors and patterns for use in drawings.

Scissors Tool can be used to do a free-form cutout. You should use the Scissors tool when you want the cutout to follow an object's contours.

 Pick Tool used to do a rectangular cutout. You should use the Pick tool when you don't need the cutout's size and shape to be precise, or if you want the cutout to be a rectangle.

 Airbrush "spray" paints in the drawing area.

 Text Tool types text in the drawing area.

 Color Eraser changes portions of the foreground color to the background color, or to change every occurrence of one color to another color.

 Eraser changes the portions of the drawing area that the cursor touches to the background color.

 Paint Roller fills a closed area with a foreground color.

 Brush paints the drawing area.

 Curve draws a curved line.

 Line draws a line.

 Box draws boxes with straight corners.

 Filled Box draws filled boxes.

 Rounded Box draws boxes with rounded corners.

 Filled Rounded Box draws filled rounded boxes.

 Circle/Ellipse draws a circle or ellipse.

 Filled Circle/Ellipse draws a filled circle or filled ellipse.

 Polygon draws polygons from connected straight lines.

 Filled Polygon draws filled polygons from connected straight lines.

Drawing a Paintbrush Graphic

1 Start Paintbrush by double-clicking on its icon in the **Accessories** group.

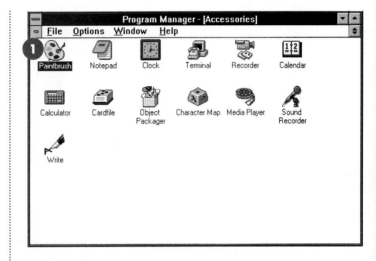

2 Use the mouse to point to the tool in the Toolbox, and click on the tool you want to use to draw.

3 Use the mouse to point to the color in the Palette that you want to use for a background color, and then click it using the right mouse button.

4 Use the mouse to point to the color in the Palette that you want to use for a foreground color, and then click it using the left mouse button.

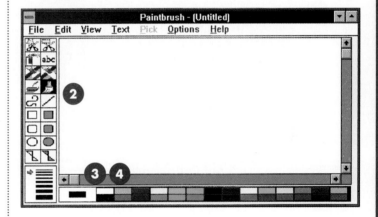

LEARNING THE LINGO

Cutout: An area of a Paintbrush drawing you can select by either using the Scissors or Pick Tool.

Windows Accessories

DRAWING A PAINTBRUSH GRAPHIC

5 Use the mouse to move the cursor to the place on the drawing area where you want to start drawing.

6 Drag the cursor around the drawing area to create the drawing, and then release the mouse button.

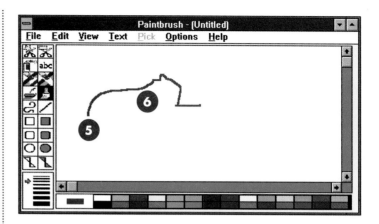

Exercise

To practice drawing in Paintbrush, draw a blue-filled rectangle in the middle of the drawing area. Use a white background (default).

1 Select the **Filled Box** tool in the Toolbox.

2 Select **White** as the color in the Palette that you want to use for the background color. (By default this will be selected when you start up Paintbrush).

3 Select **Blue** as the color in the Palette that you want to use for the foreground color.

4 Move the cursor to the center of the drawing area.

5 Drag the cursor around the drawing area to create the rectangle.

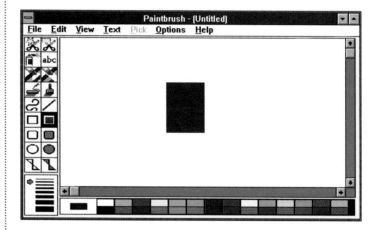

ADDING TEXT TO A PAINTBRUSH GRAPHIC

Why Add Text to a Paintbrush Graphic?

You can add titles and descriptions to your Paintbrush drawing by selecting the Text tool. You can also select the color of the text and the font type and size, in addition to formats such as bold, italic, and underline. However, you must select those attributes, prior to typing.

The Text menu allows you to select formats for the text.

Cancels bold, italic, underline, outline, and shadow character styles.

Changes the character style to bold.

You select the text tool to type text in the drawing area.

Changes the character style to italic.

Underlines text.

Outlines text using the selected background color.

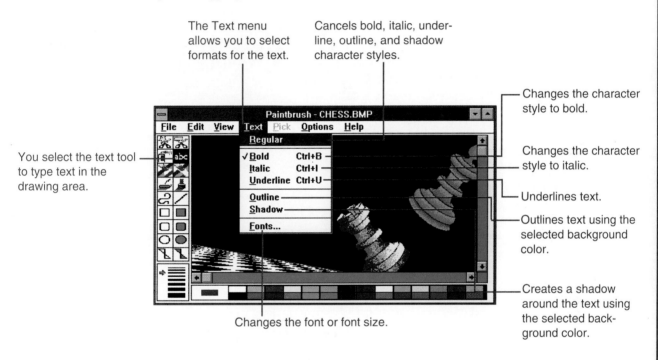

Creates a shadow around the text using the selected background color.

Changes the font or font size.

The Font dialog box appears when you select Text Fonts.

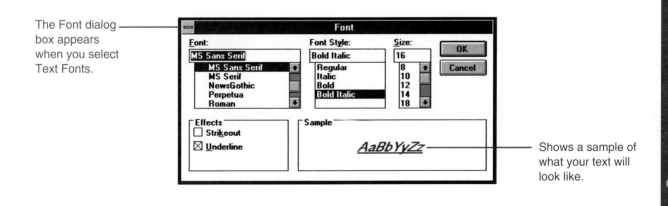

Shows a sample of what your text will look like.

127

ADDING TEXT TO A PAINTBRUSH GRAPHIC

Adding Text to a Paintbrush Graphic

1 Select the foreground color by using the mouse to point to the color in the Palette that you want to use for a foreground color, and then click on it using the left mouse button.

2 Use the mouse to point to the **Text** tool in the Toolbox at the left of the Paintbrush window, and then select it by clicking on it.

3 Point to the place in the drawing area that you want the text to appear, and then click to position the cursor. Begin typing the text.

4 To change the format of the text, click on the Text menu, or press **Alt+T**.

5 Click on the format that you want.

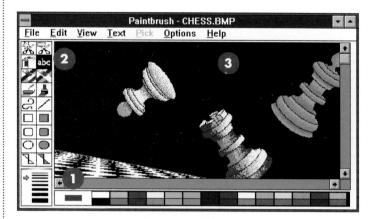

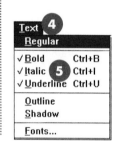

SAVING A PAINTBRUSH GRAPHIC

Why Save a Paintbrush Graphic?

Save your Paintbrush drawing so that you can use it again in the future. You can save your Paintbrush drawing in one of two types of graphic files: .PCX or bitmap (.BMP). Paintbrush is preset to save your drawing as a bitmap file. Other than selecting the type of graphics file into which to save your drawing, the steps for saving a Paintbrush file are the same as for saving Write documents or the documents of any Windows application.

File name of the drawing to be entered here.

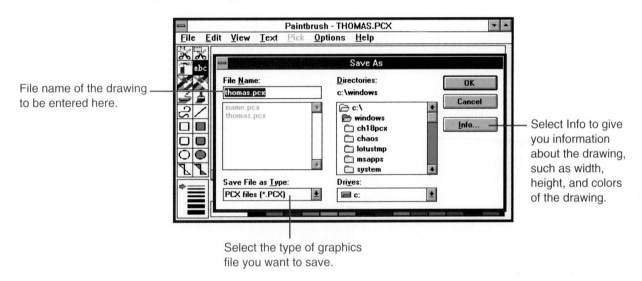

Select Info to give you information about the drawing, such as width, height, and colors of the drawing.

Select the type of graphics file you want to save.

LEARNING THE LINGO

Bitmap: A type of graphics file. Unless you specify otherwise, Paintbrush will save your file in the Bitmap format.

PCX: An alternative type of graphic file that can be used in a variety of applications.

Windows Accessories

SAVING A PAINTBRUSH GRAPHIC

Saving a Paintbrush Graphic

1 Click on File, or press **Alt+F**.

2 Click on Save As, or press **A**.

3 Type a file name in the File Name text box.

4 In the **Directories** list box, click on the directory to which you want to save the file. Or press **Ctrl+D**, and use the down arrow key to select a directory.

5 If you don't want to save the file in the default type (bitmap), click on the down arrow of the Save File as **Type** box to display other file types, and then click on the file type of choice. If you are using the keyboard, press **Ctrl+T**, and use the down arrow key to select a file type.

6 Click on the **OK** button, or press **Enter**.

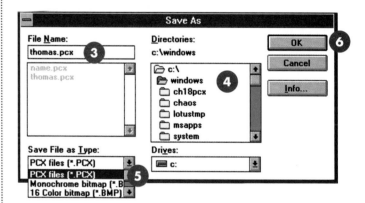

Installing Windows

To install Windows means to set the program up on your hard drive by copying certain files from the Windows 3.1 diskettes. The installation program also searches your hard disk for applications that can be used with Windows. Program-item icons are created and associated with these programs so that once Windows is set up, you can start your applications by choosing the icons. Installation should take no more than 30 minutes.

There are two methods for installing Windows: Express Setup and Custom Setup. Microsoft recommends the Express Setup method for most users. Express Setup is a program that can identify your hardware and software and then install Windows so that it will run properly with your system. Microsoft recommends the Custom Setup only for advanced users who want to alter the standard Windows installation to meet their specific needs. When you use Custom Setup, you have to provide information about your system, such as the type of computer, display monitor, mouse, printer, keyboard, and keyboard layout. The steps that follow assume that you will use the Express Setup.

1 Turn on your computer and display monitor.

2 Insert installation Disk 1 in your disk drive.

3 At the DOS prompt, type the letter of the drive containing the installation disk, followed by a colon, and press **ENTER**. For example, if you put Disk 1 in drive A, type **A:** and press **ENTER**.

4 Type **setup**, and press **ENTER**.

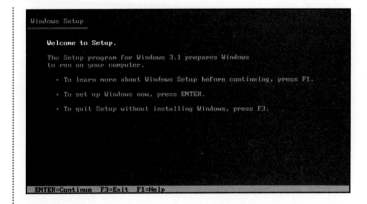

INSTALLING WINDOWS

5 Press **ENTER** again.

6 To choose Express Setup, press **ENTER**.

7 To use the suggested directory in which Windows will be installed, press **ENTER**.

8 If an earlier version of Windows is detected by the setup program, you will be asked if you want to upgrade the current version of Windows. If that message is displayed, press **ENTER**.

9 Once files have been copied from Disk 1, the setup program will ask you to insert Disk 2. Remove Disk 1, insert Disk 2, and press **ENTER**.

10 After the setup program copies more files, you will be prompted to enter your name. Type your name in the **Name** box. If you also want to enter your company name, press **TAB** to move the insertion point to the **Company** box, and type your company's name.

11 Press **ENTER**.

12 If the information on the screen is correct, press **ENTER**. If you need to make changes, click on the **Change** button, and make the changes.

13 You will be prompted to insert Disk 3 through 6.

14 Once all the files from disk 6 have been copied, the Exit Windows Setup dialog box is displayed, press **ENTER**. The installation is complete.

Glossary

active window   A window you are currently using or have selected. Only one window can be active at one time.

application   A program such as word processing, spreadsheet, or database.

bitmap   A graphical image stored in a file and made up of a pattern of dots.

cascading menu   A menu that opens from a command of another menu.

command   A word or phrase in a menu that you select to carry out a task.

Control menu   Menu of commands to manipulate windows (such as restore, move, size, and close).

Control Panel   A Windows application that provides you with a visual way of modifying your system while working with Windows.

copy   To select text or objects and use the Edit Copy command to place a duplicate on the Clipboard so that it can be pasted to another location in the document or into another application by using the Edit Paste command.

cutout   An area of a Paintbrush drawing you can select by either using the scissors or pick tool.

cutting   To select text or objects and then use the Edit Cut command to remove the item from the document and place it on the Windows Clipboard.

desktop   The screen areas on which windows and icons are displayed.

device   A component of a computer system's hardware, such as a modem, printer, mouse, keyboard, sound card, and disk drive.

dialog boxes   Windows that appear to request additional information or provide additional command options. In addition, a dialog box may ask you to confirm that you want a particular command carried out and may remind you of the consequences of the command.

directory   The structure of a disk. The way that disks are divided up. Directories contain files and other directories called subdirectories.

document   What you create with your applications, such as letters, reports, spreadsheets, or drawings.

DOS (disk operating system)   A software that resides in the computer's memory at all times and manages memory, devices, and tasks.

DOS prompt   A symbol that indicates that the operating system is ready to accept a command from the user.

double-click The action of pressing the mouse button twice in rapid succession. Double-clicking carries out an action such as starting an application or maximizing a window.

drag Point to an item, then press and hold the mouse button as you move the mouse, thereby dragging the item around the display. When finished dragging, release the mouse button.

drive A device for saving and retrieving information on disk. A drive reads from and writes to a disk.

ellipsis Three periods (...) that follow a command in a menu indicating that a dialog box will appear when you choose the command.

extension A period (.) and up to three characters that can be added to the end of a file name. For example, the file MEMO could be named MEMO.TXT to show that the file contains text (TXT).

file properties The command line (path), working directory, and program-item icon associated with a particular file.

fonts Characters of a given size and design. For example, this is a font called Courier and is 12 points in size.

graphical user interface (GUI) A graphical environment that makes the computer intuitive and easier to use.

group A collection of applications or documents within Program Manager.

group icon A small picture that represents a group of applications of documents in Program Manager.

group window A window that displays the items in a group within Program Manager.

hard disk The permanent storage area of your computer. You can use the hard disk just as you use floppy disks to save files and store applications.

icon A small picture that represents a program group, application, document, or other element of Windows.

insertion point An on-screen, flashing vertical bar where you can enter text.

jumps Links that you can click on (or select and press ENTER) to display a Help topic.

key combination Two keys that you press together to execute a task.

list of groups The names of all groups that are listed at the bottom of the Window menu.

memory The working storage area of your computer. The size of your computer's memory, also referred to as RAM (random-access memory), determines the size and number of applications that you can run at the same time and the amount of data your computer can process quickly.

moving   To select text or objects and reposition in the document by using the Edit Copy and Edit Paste command.

Paintbrush   A drawing program found in the Accessories group.

pasting   To transfer contents of the Clipboard (text or objects) into a document by using the Edit Paste command.

PCX   An altenative type of graphic file that can be used in a variety of applications.

PIF (personal information file)   A file that contains information about a non-Windows application that Windows needs to run the application within the Windows environment.

point   To move the mouse, position the mouse pointer on an item of choice.

point size   The height of a printed character. There are 72 points in an inch.

program group   A collection of applications that are displayed as icons in a window.

program item   An application or file that is represented by an icon in a program group.

Program Manager   The foundation of the Windows program that you can use to organize applications into logical groups, to start programs, and to exit from Windows. When you start Windows, the Program Manager is automatically up and running, and it is the first thing you see.

pull-down menus   A menu of choices that is displayed when its title is selected. For example, when the Windows **F**ile menu is selected, the following choices are displayed on the menu: **N**ew, **O**pen, **M**ove, **C**opy, **D**elete, **P**roperties, **R**un, and E**x**it Windows.

root directory   The top level directory of a disk.

select   To mark a word, sentence, paragraph or other item in a document.

selection area   An invisible section of the Write window that extends vertically along the left margin. You can click on this area to select text.

selection letter   The underlined letter of a menu command.

scroll   To move through parts of a window to view additional information.

scroll bar   A bar that appears at the right edge or bottom of a window whose contents are not entirely visible.

subdirectory   A directory within a directory.

syntax   A specified way that a command must be entered.

system time   The time, as kept by the computer's internal clock.

Wallpaper   An image that is displayed on the desktop background.

window   A rectangular-shaped area that displays application or document icons.

word wrap   A feature of word processing programs that allows you to keep on typing when you reach the end of a line. The application automatically moves to the beginning of the next line without you having to press ENTER or return, as you would if you were using a typewriter.

Index

Symbols

* (asterisk) wild card character, 86
+ (plus sign) in directory icons, 65
? (question mark) wild card character, 112
... (ellipsis), 14, 134

A-B

active window, 29, 31-32, 133
applications, 1, 29, 133
    icons, 12, 40-43, 28
    non-Windows, 28
    Paintbrush, 53, 123-130, 135
    running, 28, 29, 30
    Setup, 131-132
    switching between, 33-34
    Write, 108-122
attributes, 67
AUTOEXEC.BAT file, 13
automatic Windows startup, 13

Bad command or filename message, 13
batch files, 13
bitmap (.BMP) files, 53, 129, 133

C

capturing screens, 49
cascading menus, 14-15, 133
characters, formatting, 121-122
check boxes, 17-18
clicking, 8, 16
Clipboard, 47-49, 116-120
collapsing directories, 64-65
color schemes, 50-52
colors, changing on-screen, 50-52
command buttons, 17-18
commands, 15, 133
    ... (ellipsis), 14
    Character menu, 121-122
    check marks beside, 14
    Control menu, 21
    Control Switch To, 33-34
    dimmed, 14
    Disk Format Disk, 87-88
    Disk Select Drive, 61
    Edit Copy, 118-120
    Edit Cut, 116-120
    Edit Paste, 118-120
    Edit Undo, 117
    File Copy, 77-78
    File Create Directory, 70-71
    File Delete, 40-41
    File Exit, 59
    File Exit Windows, 25
    File Move, 44-46, 81-83
    File New, 35-37, 39
    File Open, 102-103
    File Print, 104-105
    File Properties, 42-43
    File Rename, 74-75
    File Save, 106-107
    File Save As, 106-107, 129-130
    File Search, 84-86

Find Go To Page, 111
Find Repaginate, 111
Find Replace, 112-113
Help menu, 23-24
Move Program Item, 45-46
Options Printer Setup, 94-96, 98-99
Options Save Settings on Exit, 25
selecting, 14-16
selection letters, 15
SETUP, 131
syntax, 135
Text menu, 127-128
Tree menu, 65
triangles beside, 14
View menu, 66-68, 91
Window menu, 79-80
WIN, 13
computer components, 6-9
Control Panel, 50-55, 133
Control-menu box, 17, 25, 30, 33-34
copying, 133
    files, 76-78
    text, 118-120
CPUs (central processing units), 7
cursor movement keys, 110
Custom Setup, 131
cutouts, 125, 133
cutting, 116-120, 133

D

dates, modification, 67
default printer, 97, 99
deleting
    icons, 40-41
    print jobs from queues, 92-93
    text, 116-117
desktop, 12, 133
    changing wallpaper, 53-55
    saving settings, 25
devices, 133
dialog boxes, 15, 17, 133
    Browse, 38
    closing, 17
    Copy, 77-78
    Create Directory, 70-71
    Desktop, 54-55
    elements, 17-18
    Exit Windows, 25
    Font, 121, 127
    Format Disk, 87-88
    Go To, 110-111
    Move, 81-83
    Move Program Item, 44
    moving, 17
    New Program Object, 35-37, 39
    Open, 102-103
    Print, 104-105
    Printer Setup, 94-96
    Printers, 97, 99
    Program Group Properties, 42
    Program Item Properties, 37-39, 42-43
    Rename, 74-75
    Replace, 112-113
    Save As, 106-107, 129-130
    scroll bars, 19-20
    Search, 23, 84-86
    Task List, 33-34
directories, 9, 60, 64, 133
    creating and naming, 69-71
    expanding and collapsing, 64-65
    listing files, 66-68
    opening multiple windows, 79-80
    root, 69, 135

    selecting, 62-63
    subdirectories, 60, 64, 135
Directory Tree, 58, 62, 64
disk drives, 7
disks
    floppy, 9, 87-88
    hard, 9, 12, 134
documents, 102, 133
    opening, 102-103
    printing, 104-105
    saving, 106-107
DOS (disk operating system), 133
DOS prompt, 133
double-clicking, 8, 134
dpi (dots per inch), 96
dragging, 16, 44, 134
drawing graphics, 123-126
drives, 58, 60-61, 134
drop-down list boxes, 17-18

E-F

exiting
    dialog boxes, 17
    File Manager, 58-59
    Print Manager, 93
    Windows, 25
    windows, 30
expanding directories, 64-65
Express Setup, 131-132
extensions, 106, 134

File Manager, 58-59
files, 8-9
    attributes, 67
    AUTOEXEC.BAT, 13
    batch, 13
    bitmap (.BMP), 53, 129, 133
    copying, 76-78
    icons, 28
    listing in directories, 66-68
    moving, 81-83
    naming, 106-107
    PCX, 129, 135
    PIF (personal information file), 135
    properties, 42-43, 134
    renaming, 74-75
    searching for, 84-86
    selecting multiple, 72-73
    sorting for display, 67
floppy disks, 9, 87-88
fonts, 122, 134
formatting
    floppy disks, 87-88
    text, 121-122

G-I

graphics
    adding text, 127-128
    drawing, 123-126
    resolution, 96
    saving, 129-130
groups, 29, 36, 134-135
    creating, 35-36
    icons, 12, 40-43, 28-29, 134
    list of, 31, 134
    moving program items between, 44-46
    windows, 12, 28-29, 134
        switching between, 31-32
GUIs (graphical user interfaces), 134

hard disks, 9, 12, 134
Help, 22-24